RESILIENCE:

Today's Pain

Tomorrow's Empowerment

5 steps to mindfully manage

anxiety, crisis, and trauma

I0532397

W WESTCOTT

CONTENTS

INTRODUCTION

Does it seem impossible to see through your life-altering illness or that of a loved one? Maybe you can't stop the negative spiral, are in a constant state of anxiety, or you anticipate a catastrophic event, regardless of whether it might happen. Perhaps a traumatic event has shaken you to your core, and you're ravaged with worry or PTSD, unable to see the light at the end of the tunnel. Do you think these feelings are all immutable facts of your life, and you will never get through them?

Well, think again.

You are capable of persevering and coming out on the other side with a new sense of calm and resilience, being all the better for it. How do I know this, you ask?

I have done the work of discovery and recovery. I have researched and understood the teachings of wise spiritual guides and successful leaders worldwide. Knowledge of the fundamentals of the mind-body connection has influenced how I live my life for the better, and I will show you how these concepts can seamlessly align with your daily life.

Most importantly for you, my years of personal experience have allowed me to understand that the lows of life are not only surmountable but beneficial to you as you develop coping skills and a steady demeanor. The tools I am about to share with you will be invaluable improvements in your life. You will radiate peaceful self-control, which will positively impact you and those around you.

I hope that sharing first-hand encounters with the depths of emotional and physical pain, which you will discover, I have plenty of, will provide the value of emotional perspective. If I overcame the trials and tribulations and confidently emerged stronger for it, so can you.

So when life backs you into a corner and you feel there is nowhere to go, no one to turn to, and when you are overwhelmed with anxiety or fear, this book will teach you exactly where to go- inward. Your resilience lives within you, and this guidebook will show you how to tap into it in five easy-to-follow steps.

Resilience is a living state of readiness that allows us to respond with the ultimate flexibility to any circumstance. Having resilience means you can recover from whatever difficulties come your way. It is not only about mental toughness but also the ability to manage painful, stressful situations and bounce back. This book will show you how to do so with a peaceful demeanor. A steady, resilient frame is armor for your soul, using the past and present as protection from future deep wounds.

Now it's your turn to redefine self-love by facing what has influenced you and created your fears. You will turn your test into a testament to your resilience. The reflections, quotes, modern methods, and easy-to-understand psychology in this book will help guide you on this journey.

It's time to move forward by facing what hurts, permitting yourself to heal, and embracing the small victories along the way. You will see your growth daily as your past will no longer define you. Instead, you will acknowledge, learn from, and thrive with your newfound strength.

The truth of life is there is "no back door." In my tale of tragedy and triumph throughout the daily "norms" of life, I felt isolated and alone in my struggles. Like many people, or unlike many people for that matter, my life has been a series of tragedy after tragedy, upheaval after upheaval. I have suffered financial ruin, loss, a rare disease, month-long hospitalization, and open-heart surgery while on the brink of death. Yet here I am, standing tall and more vigorous than I could have envisioned.

How?

I taught myself about the power of resilience.

Personal strength has guided me through harrowing life events, and resilience has given me the means to adapt at every turn, bouncing back time and time again. Acknowledging what you are facing or have faced and moving forward is a crucial component of resilience. Getting straight to the point, practically identifying adversity, you begin to see it for what it is. Acknowledging pain as a universal aspect of life, you can be brief in describing your challenges, and you will see the path to overcoming them seems more straightforward and less littered with obstacles.

Crisis after crisis was heaped on me in a relatively short amount of time between 2010 and 2019. Let me share my list of traumatic setbacks that brought me where I am today:

- My six-figure salary squandered by mismanagement and subsequent financial ruin following my husband's failed business venture and real estate market crash.
- Failed twenty-three-year marriage.
- Lost relationship with daughter for five years in the morass of misunderstandings during divorce.
- Short sale of our home.
- Declaring bankruptcy.
- Working two jobs for a period, barely surpassing the poverty line.
- Eight moves between 2009-20 (housing for family pets- a blind rescue included a challenge)
- As life crumbled in chaos, I was daily custodian to ailing parents-coordinating the "dismantling" of my father's studio compound and prolific career as he experienced a slow horrific demise from ALS disease.
- Assisted with my mother's adjustment and moves following his death.
- Our family's shocking loss of a much-beloved brother from ALS two short years after my father.
- Contracting a mysterious blood disorder that infected my mitral valve (subacute endocarditis), rendering me near total organ failure, heart block and heart failure.

- A month-long hospitalization for open heart surgery to replace my severely impaired valve and install a pacemaker/defibrillator. My incredibly accomplished cardiac surgeon said I was of his top 5 worst cases.
- Intubated in intensive care, I suffered a stroke.
- Survived an assault during my recovery period, while still in heart failure, retriggering PTSD/panic attacks.

All this while keeping a brave face and stiff upper lip in an elite real estate firm where clients complain of things like not enough closet space!

There is more, but you get the picture.

For most of my adult life, I was a strong, healthy, fit, goal-oriented businessperson, maintaining a six-figure salary while raising two incredible, now successful kids. I ran a household, was an active volunteer and member of my community. My life was full of fortune and satisfaction. Being blindsided by the darker side of life could have thrown me completely off-kilter.

To summon the power to function in society and daily life as though these tragedies and crises bore down on me were the "norm", became my "norm." As you can tell, this change in events presented me with a new world, one I had to learn to navigate before it swallowed me whole. So that's what I did.

Thriving is possible, even amidst life's most challenging moments. Using my experience, I'll show you how to utilize the power of your mind for personal healing. Learning these techniques will help you stay anchored during turbulent times, transforming adversity into energy. Eventually, you will be better for all of it- more vital, calmer, and peaceful.

This book will teach you the basics of managing your emotions via the mind-body connection, help you gain valuable insights into facing the often-harsh realities of life, and enable you to recognize, utilize and maintain the power within you to adapt to change. You will have the foundation to be the strong and resilient person you are meant to be, able to face any crisis or traumatic event with calm composure.

This newfound resilience allows you to get on with the situation at hand, more productively going with the "flow" of life rather than resisting change. There will be "exercises" (I think of them as a basic primer for living in today's fast-changing world) - one at the end of each chapter. There are five in all.

This accessible 5-step guidebook will enable you to turn the pain of living into living in the powerful present moment.

Resilience: What does it mean? We will cover the basics of how anxiety, crisis and trauma affect us, how to recognize adaptability, and, therefore, the ability to build resilience.

Chapter One: Growth Mindset provides information about the growth mindset and how our brain's adaptation and change are integral to our life. Understanding the capacity to adapt is crucial as it gives us a pathway to process change or upheaval, whether that change abruptly interferes or slowly gnaws on your daily routines. The main takeaway from this chapter is the importance of awareness - looking at ourselves as objectively human, always with the capacity to learn and grow.

This chapter contains reflection in the first of five steps.

Chapter Two: Calm Mindfulness examines the topic of mindfulness and how to use it to calm our busy brains. We seek to gain a more objective view and make better decisions, transforming negative self-talk into empowering thoughts. Empowering yourself to handle negativity is essential to tap into your resilience. These are among the myriad tools powerful and resilient people use to overcome obstacles. This chapter also discusses the solutions that are always possible in managing our reactions and building our resolve. Know that you can get through to the other side!

This chapter contains the second of five steps.

***

Chapter Three: Overcoming Fear and Anxiety explores fear and anxiety as a survival response and what we can do to acknowledge our fears, facing them head-on. Avoiding fear can have a much more detrimental emotional effect. You can grow and adapt, and so does your ability to manage your traditional concept of fear. Engage with your emotions, understand how they are triggered, and acknowledge the effects of trauma to guide you where you need to be.

This chapter contains the third of five steps.

***

Chapter Four: Building Resilience Through Perspective and Gratitude examines how to build resilience by creating a healthy perspective of gratitude. By studying how we see others, daily situations, and shared experiences, we will learn to view problems as opportunities for personal growth. We must reposition ourselves using our newfound awareness, realigning our reactions with our more peaceful, balanced worldview.

This chapter contains the fourth of five steps.

Chapter Five: Maintaining Resilience concludes with advice to help you develop and maintain resilience in your life. We will address the process of how to make changes in our lives and how to stay motivated on this new path. Applying all the concepts in this book will equip you with the tools you need to develop lasting resilience. You will be able to engage with uncertainty on a new level and approach unexpectedly harsh situations with acknowledgment of your strength, which will resonate throughout many aspects of your life and those around you. You will revel in the improvements in your life as you radiate calm composure and fortitude.

This chapter contains the last of the five steps.

Chapter Six: Ideas to keep in mind for stability and continued health- mental, spiritual, and physical.

This book provides a comprehensive yet simple-to-read guide to developing resilience in your life, helping you face your anxiety and look at crisis or trauma with bold new eyes. Consider this book a holistic primer for living with the uncertainty of our times.

What this book is not- is a lot of lists of scientific data. It does, however, rely on the mountains of invaluable research by established professionals in the fields of psychology and neuroscience and is noted accordingly. It also contains wisdom from some of the most profound spiritual leaders of our day.

While reading, you will be encouraged to apply the concepts presented in each chapter as a tool in your journey, resulting in a life filled with more personal fulfillment and more happiness. The road to resilience starts with understanding that the nature of our problems is that we expect certainty. Remembering life is a series of challenges with obstacles, we learn to prepare for and develop practical solutions.

Time and time again, I have proven myself resilient in the face of tragedy—ask anyone around me. I am genuinely passionate about sharing my knowledge with you because I know from first-hand experience that the advice I have to share is life-changing in the best of ways. You can adapt to face even the most difficult situations with steadfast resolve. If I can do it, you can too. Don't doubt yourself. You can get through whatever challenges you face, bouncing back, better for having made it to the other side.

So, let's get on with it.

Let's start you on your path to powerful...

RESILIENCE

You have the strength within you to overcome whatever comes your way.

Let's begin our journey to resilience by sorting out the basics, starting with resilience itself.

Resilience

What does it mean? You're sure to understand the word, but how does it apply to your daily life? According to the American Psychological Association (2022), resilience is the process and outcome by which a person successfully adapts to and perseveres through complex and challenging life experiences. One of the main components defined by resilience is emotional and psychological flexibility: in other words, the ability to accept whatever life throws at you or whatever crisis, accident, or event comes your way and adapt your thinking and behavior.

Cultivating specific skills can significantly increase your resilience based on these three main factors: our realistic view of the world, coping strategies implemented to aid us through difficult times, and our social skills and communication quality.

Garnering a more realistic and objective worldview is essential to resilience. If we can view the world around us with less emotional investment and a more logical, observational focus, disastrous situations and events are less likely to instill fear, anxiety and panic in us. Understanding and accepting the uncertainties of life is the key to coping, managing emotions, and "getting on with it."

Different coping strategies work for different people, but an overall ability to acknowledge when we are struggling with panic and then implement an activity or distraction process is a practice we can learn. Understanding ourselves and our reactions on such a deep level makes us less susceptible and more stable against the harshness of life. Recognizing our vulnerabilities is one aspect of the complex characteristics we rarely visit. Stepping back, conscious that you have the flexibility to adapt, disengage and distract yourself, is key to resilience.

Finally, social skills and communication play a surprisingly significant role in building and cultivating our resilience. We can relate to the emotions of those around us yet detach. We can empathize and share experiences. These human connections enable us to have a deeper understanding of our vulnerabilities and tendencies. Recognizing these commonalities plays a vital role in how we react to complex challenges and traumatic events.

These three factors form the basis of this book, providing in-depth explanations and advice on how the components of resilience fit together to create a more vital, more adaptable you.

Each and every time you push through a traumatic event and rebound, you gain more strength and build more resilience, which is essential to coping and thriving in this fast-changing world.

Suffering exists as real as you or me. It is as immutable as the sky is blue, as the gravity that keeps us grounded. Sometimes there is just no way to avoid suffering. It is here whether we anticipate it or not. Some of the most profound thinkers and teachers extoll the importance of accepting suffering as a part of human life and the fact that everything is imperfect and impermanent.

Of course, this can sound rather gloomy and pessimistic, but accepting the facts as natural as living and breathing can improve your ability to take meaningful action and move forward as naturally as taking a step forward. Consider the enlightened Buddhist principles regarding Dukkha.

The concept of Dukkha forms the foundation for Buddhism, with the word 'Dukkha' summarizing physical, mental, and psychological suffering, anxiety, and dissatisfaction (St Joseph, 2020,) whether that be suffering linked with the physical body, the ever-changing world, where things inevitably slip away from us or lack of satisfaction with our lives. In theory, to end suffering, we must only develop insight into the nature of Dukkha. Dukkha is essential to Buddhist teachings because it is the first of the Four Noble Truths of life. Suffering exists, and awareness is the way through it to an awakened state. So, we know that suffering is real and inescapable. So how does the concept of Dukkha tie into resilience?

We've established the fundamental teaching that to tackle our problems, we must first acknowledge them. Once we truly know what we are facing and see the bigger picture, we can address it more accurately and effectively. The reality is we suffer because we expect security and certainty. We suffer because we attempt to avoid suffering. We must face and embrace uncertainty.

The next of the four noble truths, Samudaya, tackles this concept, as it reflects the truth of the origin of suffering is the desire to avoid suffering. Next, we have Nirodha, which you can think of as stopping craving and breaking the cycle of suffering. Magga is the knowledge that there is a path to end this suffering if only we look for it (BBC Bitesize, 2022.)

Whether you follow Buddhism or not, the value of the Four Noble Truths teachings is unquestionable. To build resilience is to accept not only our suffering but that it has an origin, an end, and a path through it. This is not saying pain will disappear. You can handle your fears and pain and, in turn, help lead those around you by example. You can be the proverbial light at the end of the tunnel.

Anxiety, Crisis and Trauma:

To learn resilience, let's take a quick look at what we face nearly every day.

The emotion of anxiety is normal. We all have worries of varying degrees. Anxiety is the common thread to trauma and crisis- particularly at the outset of an event. When anxiety is persistent worry, all-consuming, and gets worse over time, it can be overpowering, debilitating, and a disorder. Learning to control our anxious feelings before the anxiety is heightened is just one of the tools you will learn in this book.

The fact is that none of us will get through life without anxiety on some level and some form of trauma or crisis.

About 6 of every 10 men (or 60%) and 5 of every 10 women (or 50%) experience at least one trauma in their lives. Women are more likely to experience sexual assault and child sexual abuse according to US Department of Veterans Affairs.

Trauma is the lasting effect from living through something distressing or disturbing. There are three types of trauma; acute, which results from a single incident, chronic, which is repeated or prolonged such as domestic violence or abuse. Complex trauma is exposure to varied and multiple events- of an invasive nature. A Crisis is an acute emotional upset or disruptive situation to normal functioning. (Early Connections Care MO. gov)

Are you experiencing anxiety now? Do you worry about events that may or may not happen on a daily basis? Or perhaps something devastating happened to you, a sudden death of someone close to you, or an accident occurred. Did you feel a sense of shock or denial? In the weeks following this shocking event, or during this experience, if it was long-lasting, maybe you even suffered from erratic emotions. These flashbacks likely interrupted your sleep, and perhaps you felt physically drained. If so, there's a good chance you've experienced trauma in your life already (American Psychological Association, 2022.) Trauma is not just a psychological response: it can significantly impact our mental, emotional, and physical health.

These feelings are a natural response to a severe event that changes your perception of the world. A crisis, such as a natural disaster, an accident, an unexpected and potentially life-threatening diagnosis, or upheaval, will undoubtedly bring up feelings such as sudden overwhelming, intense, and jarring pain. These feelings can prevent us from moving on with our lives, trapping us in an endless cycle of reliving the event. The event can affect our entire being- physically, emotionally, mentally, and subconsciously if we relive it repeatedly. We can harness the strength to manage our pain so that the ongoing change in life- with or without your consent! - can be faced with resolve.

With a system in place to improve our adaptability, learning to cope and thrive despite the anxiety, these situations, and life, in general, will become that little bit easier. Resilience is our capacity to adapt to adversity, whether in the form of a breakdown, disruption or painful event. Therefore, readying yourself for the future, hurt, pain, and anxiety will take a lesser form.

Adaptability:

In the first few years of life, more than 1 million new neural connections are formed every second. After this period of rapid proliferation, connections are reduced through a process called pruning so that brain circuits become more efficient. Emotional well-being and social competence provide a strong foundation for emerging cognitive abilities, and together they are the bricks and mortar that comprise the foundation of human development. (Harvard. Edu 2022) If we are fortunate, we have comfortable surroundings, love, and attention to our needs which positively affects our brain's evolution. As we progress through childhood and into adulthood, the concepts of our lives become more solidified, determining who we are as a person and how we react to situations, good or bad—basic stuff.

Our genetics and DNA provide our brains with a blueprint for our development. Our minds' structure is mapped by the world around us and our experiences. We know this. However, did you know that even with age, your brain is still capable of change? While neural pathways are established (courses of thought, action, and reaction carved over and over again through habit), these circuits can be rewired in a different direction so to speak, with consideration and practice.

In other words, new thought patterns can be rewritten. It is our choice to shift and change these patterns.

I love the analogy of training my blind dog. At first, it was easy to train him to fetch the ball with treats as a reward. Food is an easy motivator we all know. When he began to get distracted and did not always return with the ball directly, finding something occasionally more "yummy" (gross) in the yard, I decided to find a better strategy. I started clapping every time he picked up the ball so he not only knew right where I was located but also felt positive accolades. He also knew every time I received the ball, I immediately threw it out to him to race after. This new method became infinitely more effective than fumbling for food every time when he didn't know the ball would be pitched out to him again. Turns out the dog responds to positive momentum. This new method took some time and perseverance for him to learn and patience for me to teach, but has proven gratifying for him and for me. This simple example shows that with persistence and focus, we can align along the more desirable pathway, creating a new and effective pattern.

With new patterns of thought and behavior, you can tap into your inner strength, persevering through any life-changing event or even something catastrophic by learning unwavering direction and control. Our brain's ability to mold and adapt, building new neural pathways to replace old ones, is called neuroplasticity. The brain is continually transforming itself day by day. We can find it within ourselves to directly manage this transformation through our mindful practices. In this case, we can enhance our resilience, rewiring the brain from a state of panic and fear to one of quiet determination.

Our brains are truly extraordinary. Different pathways form and fall dormant, are created, and are discarded, according to our experiences. When we learn something new, we create new connections between our neurons. We rewire our brains to adapt to new circumstances. This happens on a daily basis, but it's also something that we can encourage and stimulate. (Positive Psychology Ackerman 2018)

According to Menezes Guimaraes et al (2020), the brain's structure and function are constantly affected by our surroundings, whether learning a new skill, moving in our ever-changing environment, or even meeting a new person. As a result, the environment shapes our brains, and as such, our brains' communication can be weakened or strengthened depending on various life events.

There are myriad factors that affect our behaviors and emotional responses. There can be complex chemical, biological, epigenetics, and other factors which impact resilience and adaptability. For purposes of this book and your journey here, we are focusing on the most widespread association affecting most of us. This content will primarily be based on the developmental environment which is crucial to determining our vulnerability and resilience.

If you are reading this book, chances are serious adverse events in your childhood or in your current life negatively affected you. The development of your stress responses may have been disrupted and possibly caused long-lasting damage. As we experience something traumatic, our brain takes note of the situation. Over time, we learn to notice patterns and recurrences, whether these patterns are objective or subjective interpretations from our subconscious mind. As time goes on, we become accustomed to these patterns and behaviors. We see things we are used to seeing and reacting in ways we are accustomed to responding. Emotionally charged events can even change how our brains interpret situations, shifting our entire paradigm. These changes, in turn, end up modifying our behaviors.

Trauma's impact is profound. According to the Independence Center, trauma elicits a sense of helplessness that may stay with a person for a long time. Some people carry a weight of shame or guilt from their experience and suffer from eroded self-worth. Some survivors say that they have experienced what feels like emotional or spiritual death. Chronic health problems can occur as a result of extreme stress on the body. Traumas can cause physical or psychological disabilities. Post-traumatic stress disorder (PTSD) is considered a mental health disability. It develops in people who experience symptoms with extreme intensity over a long time.

Everyday interactions and tasks can be difficult to impossible for a person living with post-traumatic stress. The good news is that while the impact of trauma is destructive, recovery is possible. We can use our adaptability to change our brains in a positive direction in the aftermath of trauma (Batz 2018) by the process of Neuroplasticity.

A typical, everyday example of neuroplasticity is meeting someone new. This introduction is the first time you've seen this person, and you have yet to learn their name. By the end of the day, though, in most cases, you would easily be able to recognize their face in a crowd and likely remember their name, too. Think of how many people you recognize and names you remember in your entire life. Each introduction forms a new neural pathway that, if revisited frequently, remains solid and stable. This is just one small example of a neural pathway formed in your brain, strengthened further by repetition and commitment. Transformations like this- big or small happen every day. Remarkable when you think about it.

Neuroplasticity provides the foundation for building resilience and learning how to cope and thrive in adversity. Not only does neuroplasticity make changes in the brain's functions, but it can also offer the potential for psychological change. (Ackerman, 2018.)

This psychological adaptability leads us to the concept of a growth mindset. Through sustained effort, someone with a growth mindset knows and believes in the ability to become a better person, whether emotionally, intellectually, or physically. This open-minded growth potential is the core of neuroplasticity. As Ackerman (2018) writes, "you might say that a growth mindset is simply accepting the idea of neuroplasticity on a broad level."

So, we now know the basics of resilience and that adaptability is a considerable component in allowing ourselves to adjust to traumatic experiences and succeed in facing adversity. Being aware of our adaptability comes with neuroplasticity and a growth mindset. But what, as it relates to resilience, is a growth mindset, and how do we utilize it to become the best version of ourselves despite facing truly challenging times?

Let's explore this further by tapping into your capacity to grow and adapt at any age.

GROWTH MINDSET

The Growth Mindset is vital in learning to heal and build resilience. But before we delve into the Growth Mindset, let's first remind ourselves of the importance of acknowledging the behavior during and as a result of past wounds.

The first step in healing something hurtful from your past is to define what it is, what happened, and how it made you feel. Bringing up painful memories can be complex because the goal here is not to relive in detail the pain experienced. Instead, the goal is to see the event for what it is- a situation that occurred and observe the behavior strategies you used to lessen the stress. Reflecting on a traumatic event or series of events as objectively as possible with less emotion is no easy feat but can have the outcome of overruling your current more sensitive perspective over time. This can be thought of as a new pathway if you will.

You've likely been viewing this hurtful memory from your inner being's point of view for a long time, but now it's time to see it from an outside perspective as an objective observer.

As you reacted to life events, you developed default responses that may not serve you well: your emotions may become internalized, your thoughts spiral out of control, and your body may feel tense and on edge. While these are natural experiences in response to a life tragedy, you have reacted this way for so long that the neural pathway is rooted and this behavior becomes as natural as breathing.

However, acknowledging this reaction as a finished product, a done deal, you can adapt your default responses into thoughts, feelings, and actions that benefit you in this process of building resilience. You may be stuck in your old ways for now, but each one of us has the incredible capacity to adapt.

So, moving forward, let's genuinely define the Growth Mindset.

The Growth Mindset:

When life's troubles come knocking on our door, it can be all too easy to retreat into ourselves and deny reality. We are often much more comfortable ignoring our issues, hoping they will go away. I more than once sought the "safety" of curling into a ball and burying my head in the sand. This false sense of comfort is short-lived and doesn't serve us in the long run. Wallowing in self-pity and not facing reality in any form is simply a deception of safety. Ignoring our problems and creating a false sense of comfort isn't serving us. Seeking temporary comfort and not facing the truth will never amount to personal growth. Being unable to adapt to situations and thrive, unable to grow and learn from our experiences because they are at times unbearable, will leave you at square one- reacting the same way over and over again. Those of us with an openness to growth take life's challenges head-on, accepting them for what they are, dealing with them with a clear open mind, knowing with certainty that this situation, too, will change.

A way to understand your current level of growth mindset might be to examine and assess how you have handled a major regret. We all have one or more. It can make you cringe, right? You wish you had made a different decision and reacted differently. Chances are it has kept you up at night. If this regret is still eating away at you, reliving this event over and over again may show a tendency away from a growth mindset.

If, on the other hand, you can envision what a more favorable outcome would look like, finding a sense of relief, you tend towards a growth mindset.

Furthermore, if you have chosen to view this regret as the past, you did the best you could at the time; you have moved on, seeing this scenario as an opportunity to learn and improve, and better for it, you show a very healthy growth mindset. Management of situations such as this defines a significant difference between someone who is more vulnerable and someone who may be more resilient.

The Growth Mindset is a rudimentary understanding of the fact that everything in life is capable of adaptation for the better. A Growth Mindset means you "thrive on challenge and don't see failure as a way to describe yourself but as a springboard for growth and developing your abilities" (Western Governors University, 2019.) Our mindset dramatically contributes to how adversity and tragedy affect us, as our reactions are within our control. Our mindset is our regulator.

Our current mindset could be ineffective in tolerating stressful situations, especially if events, no matter how big or small they may seem, cut to our core and leave us debilitated unable to process or perform. This is nothing to be ashamed of, of course. So many of us go through life without genuinely admitting the depths and effects of our traumatic events, trying to cope without delving into our behaviors and how we can change them.

A flexible mindset objectively looks at difficulties, and tragedies as part of the big picture. Removing the expectation that we should be "omnipotent" from the equation, it is possible to have a more balanced view of daily and even larger-scale stressors.

So often we find ourselves critical of our "weakness", repeating a self-effacing inner dialogue that says we should be stronger. Strengths and weaknesses coexist, and we are human for it all. To clarify, acknowledging our shortcomings is not ignoring our strengths: the two exist in tandem, and we can recognize both with a growth mindset approach which leads to positive results.

Therapists the world over use the practice of identifying strengths to build confidence in difficult times. There is evidence to show that those who know their strengths and can utilize them properly and frequently tend to feel happier, have overall better self-esteem, and are even more likely to achieve their goals in life (Therapist Aid, 2022.)

It is not easy to go from less to more- from 0 to 100- on an improvement scale. If we find difficulty in managing anxiety and stressful events, we can't just flip the switch on to cope better overnight. Let's appreciate our humanity, our strengths, and our weaknesses with zero judgment. Simply acknowledging what is, with the aim of improving our behavior one step at a time. To do this, we are taking a look at the broader view of ourselves in order to initiate new patterns.

Knowing our strengths will build confidence and self-esteem but also our ability to cope with situations that come our way. So, what power is there in acknowledging unhealthy inhibitions and weaknesses?

When we recognize our weaknesses, we say we are human and part of the human experience. We can choose to improve ourselves or become better versions of ourselves. Still, we don't fool ourselves into believing a show of strength precludes or prevents us from experiencing even the most challenging circumstances as if we are impervious. Identifying the inhibitions and habits that hold us back from embracing change and difficulties that show up on our doorstep can lead us to a straightforward approach to the future. Using this self-reflective approach and taking a quick look back through the window to the past, can help us understand and build compassion for ourselves and others and allow us to move forward.

If we feel anxious, desperate, or hopeless, these negative responses have been repeated over and over in our lifetime, reinforcing their power over us. But these responses weren't always the default. So, where did they come from?

Learning why we act the way we do is a powerful antidote to doubt and helps us progress. We can use this empathic thinking for our benefit and the benefit of the broader understanding.

One of the most significant contributing factors to an unstable emotional reaction to life events is a childhood spent in an emotionally immature home environment. We become emotionally attached to those who will most likely keep us alive—but we are otherwise blank slates, ready to learn. We learn by taking in the world around us. By doing so, we develop the ability to walk, talk, and, importantly, regulate our behaviors and emotions. We copy those around us as a means to grow and develop. This behavior is mirroring. But, as you can imagine, if we grow up in an environment with unstable parental figures, this mirroring behavior can lead us to copy the unhealthy behaviors we see around us.

Stephens (2007) writes that environmental factors during our youth can impact our impulse control, negatively affecting how we experience and react to our emotions.

The theory of mirrored behavior further details our emotional development. For example, suppose our household was one of an unstable, emotionally charged model, for instance, with an abusive parent who deals with their negative emotions by lashing out and becoming verbally and physically violent. In this case, we are more likely to display these unhealthy behavior patterns as adults.

Just as hostile environments affect us, so do positive ones. If the parental figures are educated, for example, their children are more likely to succeed than their peers with parental figures who were uninterested in educational success. You may have heard the phrase "do as I say, and not as I do" if your childhood was anything like mine. This demand's logic is debunked by behavior mirroring in children. We are much more likely to copy behavior than we ever listen to instructions. Parental actions play a significant role in how their children deal with emotional regulation and trauma, whether they mean to or not.

From generation to generation, cycles are perpetuated. Awareness of these cycles can help you to break free from them. While other factors in life come along and affect the brain's processing, parenting and childhood environments provide the basis of our learning and behavior.

What does this mean for us as we manage our emotional well-being and reactions to the realities of life? It means we can, as adults, target the source of our behavioral patterns, understand why we might behave the way we do, and work on changing our reactions from that starting point.

Capacity for Adaptability:

Built into the motor neurons in our brains is the capacity to change our reactions and behaviors. Adaptability is the ability to adjust to change and new situations. For some, it might be more challenging to alter our ways than others. Once again, this potential for transition is rooted in our childhood.

Rymanowicz (2018) suggests that we begin to show signs of high or low adaptability in childhood. Highly adaptable people find no issue or stress in adjusting from one change to another, whether changing environments or shifting activities. Taking alterations in their stride, with the acceptance that situations have changed, is armor for life, but unfortunately, for most of us, this is not standard.

Those with low adaptability will find the same situational changes difficult, showing signs of distress, and many feel a heightened sense of stress and anxiety. Most of us fall somewhere in between, grasping for a false sense of security, holding our emotions in rather than exposing our pain and fears.

In fact, according to Frontiers/Behavioral Neuroscience a phenomenon many of us may not be aware of but may be able to relate to is referred to as "stress inoculation" which shows that "humans who have been able to successfully master a mild or moderate stressor (for example, the end of a friendship or illness of a parent) appear to be resilient to a variety of other later stressors (Feder et al., 2009; Russo et al., 2012). Stress inoculation is a form of immunity against later stressors, much in the same way that vaccines induce immunity against disease (Rutter, 1993).

Consider your position on the scale of adaptability. Are you on the highly adaptable end of the scale or the low adaptability end? Have you, and do you still struggle with change, whether in place, activity, or routine? Consider also your childhood home and how the adults around you reacted to stressful situations. Can you see a pattern between their behavior and your own? Consider how the adults in your life reacted to change and difficult situations, and consider any similarities you find in your behaviors.

Regardless of your level of adaptability at the current moment, improvement is possible so there's no need to worry. With the basic exercises in each chapter and some dedication, you can become more resilient when faced with upheaval, and with more situational flexibility comes the ability to weather storms more easily.

We can start by acknowledging basic reactions to events that were out of our control. How did we maintain control, did we maintain control? The first step in this guide is simply taking a step back to see ourselves. Easy.

Step: Exercise 1

In this exercise, we will take that rearview mirror view of our coping mechanisms and stress responses. Make sure you're in a space free of stress and distraction and have the free time to complete this exercise with your full attention. You can think it through, but it might be helpful to write your thoughts down on paper. Buried ideas are much clearer and make more sense when written down.

In your own time, recall a childhood or adolescent situation where you were subject to an intense crisis or a traumatic event. This upsetting experience can be anything that gives you a sense of anxiety; an assault, a grave illness, or maybe a significant life change. How did you overcome it? Write down what you can remember, from your initial shock and sadness and then to actions as small as trying to figure out why something happened, to more targeted measures. Maybe music became your trusted companion, with your favorite songs playing over and over again. You may have just slept for extended periods of time. You may notice that some of your intuitive coping mechanisms were rooted in your basic involuntary behavior at this time in your young life. You certainly feel sympathy for this child. You likely marvel at the tenacity and bravery too. Whatever approach you took is not good or bad- it just is. Could some of these strategies be implemented into your life now?

If you can clarify specific character strengths from analyzing your coping strategies, write these down, too. For instance, if one of your coping mechanisms was perseverance, recognize this ability to prioritize and stick to your routine despite trying circumstances.

It is noteworthy if you have thoughts about how you could have handled this situation differently. How would you manage your stress levels if this were to happen again? Could you assist others around you now if something as sudden and unexpected happened again?

If you're struggling to recall how you got through the situation, take a minute to reflect that you have overcome it, no matter how. Even if burying your feelings to cope worked at the time, fine. You are here now, present, at this point in your life.

You are recalling point by point an occurrence that preceded other occurrences and you are moving on, taking lessons from all of it- good, bad, indifferent.

The reminders of Buddhist teachings in Dr Mark Epstein's eloquent Book "The Trauma of Everyday Life" states perfectly, "Facing the traumas we are made of, and the new ones that continually shape us, makes more sense than trying to avoid them, if the mind is in a balanced enough place to hold the truth."

The first step in your journey to resilience is bigger than you may think. Witnessing the development of your ability to handle stressful events is empowering. Time has worked in reverse for so many of us when it comes to coping skills and bravery. We have the ability to reverse the effects of time on our minds and therefore influence and improve our behavior.

2

CALM MINDFULNESS

We know to acknowledge our strengths and weaknesses in equal measure and have even explored how these traits and behaviors might have come about through various behavioral patterns. How do we put this knowledge into practice? How do we harness our mind's power for emotional and psychological healing? How do we notice our thoughts and behavioral patterns when overloaded with everything around us? Let me show you.

The mind can be a busy place. No matter how much you try to calm it or to distract your awareness with your daily activities, sometimes the rattling of ideas and thoughts in your head can be relentless. Particularly in today's world, the constant stream of information can be overwhelming and overwhelmingly negative.

Chances are, this overwhelment becomes exponentially more intense and bleaker after dealing with trauma, especially if you are still trying to cope with the consequences of life-changing circumstances. This is where mindfulness comes into play.

Calm mindfulness:

Calm mindfulness is the practice by which we become mindful and bring awareness to our thoughts. Through meditation, we can learn to control the number of ideas in our head minute by minute, allowing for the opportunity to create space in our minds and control our emotional reactions more accurately. Learning to do so will greatly impact how you perceive events and circumstances beyond your control, and in turn, you will be able to face life with a calm and level head.

The central concept of mindfulness is presence. Learning to focus on the here and now is a powerful experience. Gone are the thoughts of the past, and what could be, and brought into focus are your bodily sensations, the emotion that sits in your chest. Bring your attention to the world around you now, not with judgment but with objective observation. Focus on your five senses, and know that right now, at this moment, this is all that exists.

With quiet consideration, sit and contemplate your surroundings. What can you see, hear, smell, taste, and touch? Don't think too hard about this. Instead, ground yourself in the now, and see how your body and mind react.

A typical mindfulness practice that is said to calm our racing thoughts and heartbeat is to focus purely on our senses. We start with sight, naming five things we can see- which can be anything at all. Next, name four things we can hear. Then three things we can feel, two things we can smell, and one thing we can taste. This simple calming method draws our attention to our surroundings and brings awareness to the present, not the past or the future.

You can see this activity has the potential to reestablish our awareness of our mind-body connection without question or assumption. Guided imagery can do this as well. There are many great teachers and psychotherapists who are experts in this field who you may consider looking into- my favorite being Belleruth Naparstek. We will explore similar practices in more depth later in the chapter.

The simple mind-body connection is the meaning of feeling present. According to the Greater Good Science Centre (2022,), mindfulness "involves acceptance, meaning that we pay attention to our thoughts and feelings without judging them—without believing, for instance, that there's a 'right or wrong' way to feel in a given moment."

Mindfulness is the practice of simply noticing; the ability to remove your judgment from a situation and take a moment or two to look at what's happening and accept it for what it is. Once we learn to accept what is, and remove the emotion from our perception, the challenges we face don't seem quite as daunting.

So, mindfulness works in theory. It sounds great to be able to observe things from a rational perspective and feel more aware of the present. Sure. But is Mindfulness practice out of reach? No - even in the most challenging times.

The American Psychological Association (2019) has concluded that mindfulness is essentially two components: attention, where you focus on experiencing the present moment, including your surroundings and the sensations in your own body; and acceptance, where you acknowledge these observations without judgment or force, knowing they are fact. These two components, put into practice, will center your mind and your focus will become grounded, rather than scattered. This center will positively affect your ability to filter intense emotions and you can more easily manage anxiety. Feeling initial stressors, you can calmly focus rather than waiting until the height of stress to calm down and focus.

Our attention is what we notice. Our acknowledgment is simply saying, "yes, this is how things are at this precise moment." A peaceful presence will become second nature.

In over two hundred studies of mindfulness practice, the consensus is that mindfulness-based therapy reduces stress, anxiety, and depression levels in healthy individuals. In participants diagnosed with clinical depression, mindfulness hugely impacts the prevention of relapse into a major depressive episode, with participants relapsing significantly less than before their mindfulness therapy intervention.

> *"Anxiety has people trapped in their own mind— in their thoughts and emotions—whereas mindfulness frees people, allowing them to experience and accept life as it is without worrying about what bad things might happen or reading into what something might mean."*
>
> TANYA PETERSON NCC

Such a simple task can improve your mental state by leaps and bounds. Not only can mindfulness improve your mood and emotional responses, but it has been proven to improve physical health, too.

According to the APA (2019), "chronic stress can impair the body's immune system... [so] by lowering the stress response, mindfulness may have downstream effects throughout the body." By calming our minds and alleviating our thoughts of stress and panic for a few minutes a day, our body is given a rest from the hormones we inadvertently pump into it.

On the musculoskeletal level, reducing stress through mindfulness can help our body relax, releasing built-up muscle tension and slowing our heart rate. The mental and physical aspects of stress and trauma are intertwined: if we can reduce the mental symptoms, we can also reduce the physical symptoms.

It's all too easy for us to run away from our own physical experience when dealing with trauma, as most of the time, our running away allows us to hide from the issue, hoping it will go away. Experience tells me they never do. We must ground ourselves in our bodies and experience the here and now.

Physical and mental awareness is the gateway to meditation and experiencing open-minded mental relaxation.

"By using the body as a beginning focus of meditation, by gradually easing oneself into the moment-to-moment reality of physical embodiment, the mind begins to learn an alternative to dissociation."(Epstein 2013 p124). Not only can the calm mind relax the body but an awareness of the body allows a connection and awareness of the mind.

Epstein (2013, pages 124-126) further outlines the first foundation of mindfulness and how can focus on the physical to alleviate the mental. To be mindful, we must be aware of ourselves and our environment, and here is where mediation comes in.

The act of first focusing on the breath, noticing it enter and leave the lungs, the airway, the mouth, and the nose, grounds us in our physical experience. We focus on what Epstein labels the "five sense doors," which are the eyes, the ears, the mouth, the nose, and the body, noticing how each of these feels and responds to the external stimuli and surroundings. As we've already mentioned, these sense doors are the perfect gateway for redirecting our focus.

The next important step is the mindfulness of feelings. This step serves as the bridge between the body and the mind, connecting them with certainty and understanding how one inevitably affects the other. As our thoughts affect our body, our physical sensations spur on and inspire our thinking or lack thereof.

While focusing on the physical aspects of mindfulness, you may have expected we should focus more on facts by eradicating emotion. However, removing our emotional perception while being mindful is saying something other than "we should repress our feelings." To suppress our emotions is to deny further the truth, which prevents us from facing the reality of change which won't serve us well. Instead, mindfulness encourages the acceptance of emotions, too.

The ability to observe your surroundings and the situation you find yourself in without judgment is one skill; it is another to be able to observe your emotions in the same way. Don't run from them, and don't try to push them away. Instead, notice how they make your body feel —maybe your shoulders are tense, your jaw clenches, perhaps you feel nauseous, and your heart is beating quickly—and accept them as part of your now reality. There is no need to do anything with them except experience them.

Feelings flow continuously, whether positive, negative, or neutral, and as you improve your mindfulness practices, you'll notice how these feelings are in your mind and body. They are interwoven. We may feel the inclination to be drawn to pleasant emotions and dissociate ourselves from unpleasant ones. It's becoming aware of our responses to our feelings that can help us to accept and understand them. As Epstein further explains (p125) "One learns to abide in the flow of feeling, not pushing away the uncomfortable and not hanging on to the pleasurable."

Mindfulness coaxes us to view all emotions as the flow of human experience, resisting the urge to push certain emotions away or draw others closer. Instead, notice them. After a while, you will find it easier to train your attention to achieve a mental state of concentration and equilibrium.

Observing feelings without judgment is the trick to improved resilience. This is the trick to being able to hold off your response time, not getting to a height of stress level to then try to calm down. Once you emerge from letting your feelings swallow you whole to a space where you own your feelings with a calm acceptance, you are well on your way to a happier, healthier outlook on life.

Emotional Non-Responsiveness to Negative Stimuli:

So, how does this simple acknowledgment of our feelings relate to how we respond to negative stimuli?

Mindfulness helps us to not immediately react to negative stimuli. For example, in the mental space where you are now if something were to happen (or if it indeed already has,) you would be forgiven for your emotions spiraling out of control immediately. Your heart rate increases, your palms become sweaty, and suddenly your thoughts are racing so quickly that there is no longer a coherent pattern.

You are in a state of panic, and quickly your sense of the situation at hand deteriorates into one where you are trapped in your reaction. This reaction to your response is entirely normal—I have had plenty of experiences where I have reacted in this way, and the negative stimuli have threatened to ultimately send me over the emotional and psychological edge.

However, when we learn to delay our strong emotional response to a situation, and interrupt the feedback loop, we can also learn how a balanced and rational mind can help us overcome the problem as it arises and learn to navigate the (potential) months of pain that follow afterward.

One of the main components of developing an anxiety disorder, PTSD for example, revolves around our emotional reaction to the trauma as it happens. As you can imagine, in the face of danger, our body goes into a shock-like state that triggers our fight-or-flight response and overrides our mind.

In immediate danger, this response is natural, and the sharpness of this reaction should lessen as we seek our safety. However, sometimes this natural response doesn't subside, leaving our body in a state of shock for longer than is necessary. Our emotions are so strong, fear and anxiety so potent in our system, that our brains are not allowed the appropriate space to decipher, manage and make sense of the experience.

Without the space to digest, we are in emotional limbo. Our bodies are hyper-alert, and our brains unable to process the information as it presents itself around us. In this case, our emotions have overridden our brain's capacity for mindfulness and thoughtfulness. As a result, without the ability to process the traumatic experience, we are left in a state of perpetual repetition, reliving the experience moment after moment and even day after day.

Initial emotional non-responsiveness is vital in tackling how trauma affects us. When we can first assess the situation as it unfolds in as factual and objective a manner as possible, we can process what's happening before our emotions have the chance to overwhelm our unbiased judgments. I have learned to wait to respond to almost anything. My delayed and composed response was not always easy for me, by the way. Gaining perspective and learning mindfulness techniques have helped me control my reactions, waiting for a time when I can respond more effectively.

An essential factor in effectively interrupting that feedback loop by non-responsiveness is an awareness of what exact emotion it is you might be feeling, whether positive or negative. Labeling your feelings helps you to know what it is you're dealing with. In this instance, you might find it useful to understand the eight basic emotions as outlined by James Madison University Education (2022):

- **Anger**: fury, outrage, wrath, irritability, hostility, resentment, and violence.
- **Sadness**: grief, sorrow, gloom, melancholy, despair, loneliness, and depression.
- **Fear**: anxiety, apprehension, nervousness, dread, fright, and panic.
- **Joy**: enjoyment, happiness, relief, bliss, delight, pride, thrill, and ecstasy.
- **Interest**: acceptance, friendliness, trust, kindness, affection, love, and devotion.
- **Surprise**: shock, astonishment, amazement, astound, and wonder.
- **Disgust**: contempt, disdain, scorn, aversion, distaste, and revulsion.

- **Shame**: guilt, embarrassment, chagrin, remorse, regret, and contrition.

As you're practicing your mindfulness and focusing on your emotion, see if you can give it a label. Labeling emotion will clarify your response, which, as we know, is an essential factor in mindfulness. Giving a feeling a name is a step towards accepting it, and you might even find that it diminishes the power it holds over you. Have a look at the list above and see if you can relate to any of the emotions and conjure a description of the physical sensation.

It should be restated: emotional non-responsiveness is not the same as emotional repression. With emotional repression, you deny your feelings and the effect they have on you. Emotional non-responsiveness, on the other hand, uses your skill of mindfulness to take your emotion out of the equation until you grasp the situation at hand. From there, you can consider your emotions accordingly. It is about learning to not instantly react, changing your default reaction of panic to one of more careful consideration. Reducing emotion, especially when you find yourself in the midst of a negative situation will lessen the heightened energy of the moment.

Removing emotion from an issue may seem impossible. It may seem like you're being asked to change the person you know yourself to be. This may feel particularly true if you have already faced some tumultuous life events and reacted to them immediately and with intense emotions every time. However, it would help if you remembered that these actions and reactions were learned in the first place. Learned behavior can be unlearned through non-responsiveness and mindfulness. A new, healthier response can take its place. You are effectively retraining your brain. Label your emotion, and observe it for what it is: not an overwhelming, irreversible state, but a subjective reaction to internal interpretations of external stimuli.

Considering this, improving your emotional non-responsiveness can also be achieved by simply taking the time to wait before you respond. If you're facing a minor affront like a rude email that's thrown you off your stride to something more extreme, such as receiving negative news about an illness of you or a loved one, stop and wait. Take a few deep breaths, focus on the way the air feels flowing through your nose and lungs, and clear your mind.

Once you have calmed your body, consider your situation's facts, weighing the event's severity. Even wait overnight to respond so that in the light of day, you can better approach the problem in an appropriately calm manner and with clarity.

This extra time allows you to process the here and now, and your refusal to let your deep, raging emotions overtake you is a power of strength and resilience that will see you through a potential escalation. As you will experience, the smaller events, like a rude comment or email, are easily de-escalated by the conscientious pausing of your mind and emotions. Once regarded in a more balanced manner, a terse email can be ignored, responded to politely, or even addressed directly, but in an appropriate, professional way.

Admittedly there will be more difficulty in applying this practice to more devastating news. Still, more mental clarity and calmness will enable you to acknowledge the situation, confidently accept it, and prepare yourself to deal with it (emotionally, mentally, and physically) in a healthier manner.

When receiving bad news about an illness, focus your attention on the facts of your situation. Relax your body, control your breathing, and take a minute. Ask questions to clarify and objectively look at what's happening if you need to. A certain treatment isn't working, but there are many others to try that may have the desired effect. Maybe there is no known cure, but multiple people who have suffered the same illness have fully recovered, some without the intervention of medicine. These facts will become the beacons of hope and resolve in times when everything seems to be crashing down around you. Taking moments to consider will allow information to be revealed before you let your emotional response overtake you.

Our emotional reaction can send us into overdrive, often focusing purely on the negative that we face, and ignoring any facts that don't fit into our negative paradigm. Taking the time to see things without such an extreme initial unemotional reaction will balance our viewpoint, helping us process the good and "the not-so-good".

We can find more useful concepts surrounding mindfulness and meditation in Epstein's (2013, pages 89-90) brilliant guidance. He makes the important distinction between listening and thinking; observing and judging.

When noticing your surroundings, try and keep an eye on whether you are simply listening to the sounds around you, or whether these sounds trigger a thought process to start churning in your mind. If they do, as always, gently bring your attention back to your surroundings, judgment-free.

Epstein continues, "treat your mind the way you would a young child who doesn't know any better. Be gentle but firm." If we consider our own mind to currently be a free spirit, a child, we can acknowledge that it will do no good to get angry at our mind and force it aggressively to change its mechanisms. If anything, this will only serve to create more resistance when trying to control our thoughts and empty our minds.

Instead, we must treat our mind with kindness and patience, coaxing it back to a gentle focus and observation, no matter how many times it wanders. Be easy on yourself; this will get easier and easier with practice, I promise! One day, you will find that your mind barely wanders, and the amount of time your quiet mind lasts will only increase.

I also want to accentuate the importance of mindfulness being an active process rather than a passive one. "Mindfulness does not mean stewing in one's juices or merely accepting what is," Epstein continues, stating that sitting in your stillness without an active awareness of your present results in doing only that: sitting in stillness. "The active and investigative dimension of mindfulness opposes this tendency."

Don't sit passively. Notice the world around you, and notice your noticing. Investigate the world around you with your senses from a neutral perspective, and acknowledge what you are seeing, hearing, and feeling. Focus is an active process.

Step: Exercise 2

Exercise two focuses on meditation — after all, we know all the benefits of it now, so let's put it into practice. If you want a more in-depth understanding of meditation, its various approaches, and its history, there are a multitude of books that can help you to delve deeper. You can download free apps with audio directions for your phone or computer that guide you through the steps to effective meditation. The choice is yours, and there are so many different options to explore. For now, you can also follow this quick and simple guide on enhancing your mindfulness.

I find the best time of day to meditate is early in the day after you've properly woken up and gone about some of your daily tasks (like eating breakfast and brushing your teeth) but before you've truly begun to engage with the day. This way, you can catch your mind at its quietest before it's had the chance to get revved up with thoughts affected or inspired by your day's activities.

Sit or lay back comfortably in a quiet location where you're sure to be free from distractions and interruptions. You might even find it beneficial to find some form of white noise in the background if silence is too intense for you or you need something to block out other sounds, like maybe the noise of a fan or that of a white noise soundtrack on your phone or computer, for instance. (If you use your phone, make sure to turn your notifications off for the time you intend to meditate)Relax. You can keep your eyes open or closed for this, but either way, relax the muscles across your body. Now, you're ready to begin.

First, engage your breath. Breathe slowly in, noticing the air passing through your nostrils, throat, airways, and lungs. Breathe slowly out, noticing how the air travels on its journey. Repeat this four or five times, slowly, just paying attention to your breathing. If thoughts come— and they will come — notice them, but try not to engage in them.

I find it helpful to think of my thoughts like clouds. Just imagine you lying outside on a sunny day, watching the blue sky as clouds drift across. Just like the clouds will wander in and out of your field of vision, so too will your thoughts. See the cloud, accept it, and release it from your awareness as you let it drift away.

Try this for a few minutes, but remember not to force it. Simply try your best. If you struggle with letting your thoughts go or can't stop yourself from thinking, then make sure to realize and acknowledge that you are doing the best you can.

For people whose thoughts are constantly racing and spiraling in fits of panic and despair, learning to let them go is no easy feat. Applaud yourself for taking a step on this journey, knowing that the more you practice, the easier it will be to clear your mind.

Repeat the above steps, refocusing on your breathing if concentrating becomes a challenge. Gently move your awareness away from any thoughts as they arise. If you get as few as three to five minutes of little to no thought or see a humming white light, you may notice a change in your bodily sensations. Some people report the relaxing sensation of feeling as though they're floating, even if just for a second. If you feel and see these things, accept them, and say "thank you" for them. You have achieved a state of complete mindfulness and have meditated.

The next time you practice meditation, you will achieve more clarity of mind and non-thought. It's all a matter of practice, not "pressured practice." Look at this as attention to non-attention! Take some time to acknowledge your accomplishments while also bearing in mind that you will inevitably improve. Continue this practice daily with no expectations of time or otherwise and with no pressure on yourself, and enjoy the differences you see.

Remember, this book is promoting mindfulness and clarity of mind to improve your ability to accept circumstances objectively, enabling your emotions to stay in check - learning, dare I say, "patience" and therefore building your resilience to the otherwise upending experiences of life.

3

OVERCOMING FEAR AND ANXIETY

E motional regulation is the ability to control internal feelings and is one of the foundational components of resilience. Control your emotional response to the external environment, and you are halfway there.

Curbing the natural tendency to worry excessively and ruminate in response to adverse life events is complex and challenging. With mindful awareness, control becomes easier over time.

Now that you are familiar with mindfulness and the first steps you can take toward self-control, it is time to talk about coping, conquering fear, managing anxiety, and managing negativity. So you already have the mindfulness tool in your arsenal; what's next?

Let's talk about fear. It is a basic human instinct. Fear is a universal emotional response, whether in response to an immediate or anticipated danger or threat. Rational or not, it can prevent us from growing, developing and even participating in daily life. Anxiety associated with the sense of fear over time can be crippling.

What is Fear?:

In its primary sense, fear is a natural human reaction to danger intended to keep us safe from harm and is both an emotional and biochemical response (Fritscher, 2022). While fear is our protection, it can become a mental health condition with symptoms such as PTSD and phobias.

As a symptomatic emotion, fear may not appear in reaction to a real threat but rather an imagined or even subconscious one. The fear a person experiences, being hit by another driver and crashing a car, may seem vastly different from the fear a person experiences before public speaking, for example, but our innate reactions can manifest nearly the same. Fear of rejection, failure, and events, either real or imagined are undeniably emotional. We often react without thinking in times of great strife and our reaction can be elevated for no true reason.

In the example of public speaking, this fear is not the same potency. You may be uncomfortable and wish to escape the situation, but there is no sense of impending harm or threats to your life. This type of fear may be more manageable and easily controlled as rational thoughts will have more space to form. Most of our fears in day-to-day life fall into this category but there is no denying true fears in the form of oppression, war, and loss of many types can also be present in our daily lives.

Although fear varies in nature, the effect on our bodies and minds is similar. Fear can help us, make us aware, and wake us up. However, fear can often be misplaced, a natural reaction to threats we have subconsciously adapted. Identifying and managing our fear-based responses to situations in life that are not a direct threat is challenging. Fear is that four-letter word we all have; how do we deal with it?

The official statistics suggest that in the United States, well over 40 million adults (19.1%) suffer fear daily in the form of an anxiety disorder (including approximately 7% of children aged 3-17,) (National Alliance on Mental Illness 2017). However, this number is likely much higher.

A healthy sense of fear can help us keep alert and cautious to avoid dangerous situations and even help us prepare for events that might head our way. If you have experienced fear during and after a harmful or terrifying situation, you are experiencing a natural reaction to a threat. However, sometimes this fear is persistent to a point where it no longer benefits us.

Let's delve further into the fear response and how it affects our body and mind.

You may well be familiar with the term "fight or flight," with some iterations of this saying transforming it to "flight, fight, or freeze." These are the three primary fear responses that our body can trigger if we sense a threat nearby: we either face the fear head-on and attack the source of it, we run from what scares us in the hopes we can escape it, or we freeze, so struck by the fear that we cannot think or move. This reaction evolved to keep us safe when natural predators hunted humans. Our fight, flight, or freeze response remains with us as predacious threats have evaporated. We may find ourselves reacting in one of three ways to something less life-threatening, like bad news, a near-accident, or even work stress.

If these stressors are chronic, meaning their impact stays with us for an extended time, our chances of having a panic attack and developing mental health problems increase. Either way, if our stress response is triggered too often due to actual or perceived fear, a hormone called cortisol is released into the body in large quantities. In a fear reaction, cortisol aids our body in either fighting or fleeing, releasing more blood sugar and preparing your body with the energy it may need when faced with danger.

However, in everyday life, when this cortisol is released but is not necessary to counter our current situation, it can adversely affect our health. For example, large amounts of cortisol remaining in our bodies for long periods has been linked to the development of various illnesses, from heart disease to a lowered immune system response and even memory loss (DeJohn, 2022). Understanding this response and how we are more likely to react to a dangerous situation can provide another step forward in managing stress. Not only can reducing our fear response improve our mental health, but it can also help reduce the impact of fear on our physical health.

Do Not Be Immobilized by Fear:

Knowing our fear response helps us to understand why we act and react the way we do. So now that we know a little about the fear response, it is time to utilize our awareness to improve our mental and physical health by minimizing our anxiety.

Fear is a genuine emotion. Acknowledge it and remind yourself that it is okay to be fearful. Avoiding fear rather than facing it can eventually leave you worse for wear, resulting in more intense emotions later. What is the point of worrying about the unknown when we can face our problems head-on? The following few paragraphs will help you use fear to your advantage, especially if, like me, you have had one or two panic attacks in your lifetime and would like some methods to follow to prevent them or even lessen their effects.

Disclaimer: some people will need more help than this book can provide, and that is okay. If you feel that your response to fear is uncontrollable and that no self-help technique will diminish the persistent anxiety you are feeling, I encourage you to seek professional psychiatric and/or medical assistance. Professionals can tailor help and support more specific needs and traumas, and their advice can be life-changing. Call your doctor for advice or a referral.

So, let's make fear work for us.

We know that fear is the body's natural response to keeping us free from danger. However, in many instances, our body is just running on autopilot: it does not know how extreme the risk may be or whether this perceived danger is a physical threat to our livelihood. Once we have acknowledged a danger, big or small, our faithful body gets to work trying to protect us. There are times when fear is helpful to us and when it is not. With this in mind, we realize that our fear response can be altered if only we learn to reinterpret our fears in a way that benefits us.

Acknowledging that our fear response is trying to help rather than hinder us allows us to accept our feelings. Think of it like owning a noisy but well-intentioned dog. Anytime there is a knock at the front door, the dog barks suddenly and loudly, alerting you to potential danger and not stopping until it has gone. No one malicious is at the front door, but the dog does not know this: as annoying as a noisy dog would be, you know he is only barking to alert and protect you from harm.

This defense is akin to what our body's fear response is doing. It is merely trying to keep us safe and protected from potential harm. Take a minute or two to honor your fear response for trying to protect you this way, and feel the power this emotion holds, knowing it is there for your benefit.

Another consideration in making fear work to our benefit is acknowledging that fear challenges us, giving us the energy and resolve to master demanding tasks we may have thought impossible. Although fear and anxiety can sometimes reduce productivity, both can increase it if appropriately harnessed. For example, imagine you have a public speaking engagement, for example. Public speaking can be frightening and this fear of failure has often incited a sense of fear in me. What does this fear do for us? In this instance, the inclination is to take the opportunity of that nervousness and energy to prepare and rehearse to avoid mistakes. In a basic sense, this intense fear propels us to make a more concerted effort to churn out a better-prepared speech. In this hypothetical situation, we have positively honed our feelings of fear. Fear can provide the determination and drive and, in this case, even provide a positive outcome of increased self-assurance.

Although fear may have its benefits in certain situations, it can hinder us in others. For example, the distinction between what Segal (2020) calls genuine fear and manufactured fear is an important one. Learning to accept genuine fear as a benefit is a significant step forward in handling feelings of fear. However, we must also learn to contemplate our feelings and emotions and recognize when we might feel manufactured fear. Often, manufactured fear may push us emotionally, mainly when it results from someone else's agenda and not our own. Manufactured fear may also be a result of past trauma that we have been through, even though we are in no danger at all. For instance, as a young person, perhaps you were injured or diagnosed with a severe illness and hospitalized for weeks with little understanding of whether you would recover. Although you might be well now, finding yourself in a hospital environment may trigger a fear response. This reaction is an example of your brain and body keeping you safe, alerting you to a situation even if the danger is gone. Even though this fear feels very much like a response to a real danger, acknowledging that your feelings may be a manufactured response to a previous situation can help you manage your emotions. Rationalizing your feelings will help you effectively control your behavior and decision-making.

Learning about the things we fear is another way to rationalize our feelings, reducing our automatic reactions to perceived danger (Segal, 2020.) As humans, we are frequently afraid of things we do not quite understand or have not been exposed to much in our lifetimes. Researching our fear can help give us expertise and control over our emotions.

Perhaps you are terrified of flying, for example. The concept of a massive tube of metal flying through the air with no mobile wings, filled with hundreds of people, is undoubtedly one that can be difficult to get your head around—it seems to defy our understanding of how things work down here on solid ground. However, once you understand how planes work and the facts of aerodynamics, things seem less threatening. There is an excellent video of an engineering student explaining that an airplane suspended in the air is much the same as a penny suspended in a bowl of jelly. Then, all of a sudden, the aerodynamics theory made much more sense. Once you know that the chances of a plane falling out of the sky is similar to a penny just dropping to the bottom of a bowl of hard-set jelly, your fears may subside.

Knowledge is power, and in this age of information, we can explore and learn about what instinctively frightens us to a point where our sense of fright begins to make sense, and anxiety can diminish. Segal (2020) states that one of the most effective ways to conquer our fears is to distinguish whether it is useful to us. From there, we can research the topics that scare us and let real fear motivate us to be safe and face challenges head-on.

Letting Go of Fear:

Letting go of anything can be difficult, especially if we've spent much of our lives experiencing the relative comfort of the familiar. Familiarity often provides solace in our complex lives, even if this mechanism does not serve us in the long run. Fear of the future, such as letting go of marriage is a common feeling of frightful unpredictability. Not knowing future outcomes can leave you hanging on a precipice of uncertainty and plague us throughout our lives.

Everything in life is temporary. Letting go of things as they depart from our lives so we can move on with calmness and productivity is a healthy natural response to the ephemeral. Have you ever tried to hold on to something you know is slipping through your fingers? Maybe a relationship is failing, and though you can see no way to rectify said relationship, you are trying to hold on to the familiar. Maybe a project you have been working on is not progressing, and it would benefit all parties to give up and start fresh, but the amount of hard work and effort you put into it makes you more determined to work against the flow as your work crumbles around you. So think about how you feel when you refuse to let things go and accept a new reality. A sense of overwhelming helplessness develops as a fear of failure to adapt creeps in. The same can be true for not letting go of fear: the more we refuse to accept it, the more we wallow in the emotions without addressing fear's power to consume us. For this reason, letting go of the power of unnecessary fear, distress, and past life events is imperative in moving forward.

Think of it like quicksand. You have found yourself in the patch of whirling sand, enveloping you in its grasp. The more you struggle, the quicker the sand draws you down, taking advantage of panic and thrashing by dragging you down further. The more you resist, the more power it holds over you. Once you calm down and take a moment to breathe, you relax. The sand's strength begins to diminish. Eventually, you stop sinking completely. In this analogy, fighting against quicksand only enhances its strength. However, when you take consideration of the surroundings and resist the urge to fight, things have less power to control and overwhelm you.

Letting go means letting go of resistance, and much as we do in meditation and mindfulness, letting go of the expectation of a particular outcome and fear. You can be free of the clutches of fear. Les Brown summarizes this theory perfectly. He is a motivational speaker who has helped millions of people through difficult times. Letting go of fear is imperative. Brown (2021) says that the way we react to and accept or deny our fear is the "difference between having fear and the fear having you." Fear is unavoidable, but how we view it results from our flexible mindset and ability to be mindful. Denying fear is allowing it to control you. Denying fear will enable it to live in your mind daily, weekly, and monthly without being addressed or accepted. Denying fear means that fear festers within us, builds, and grows until it is with us every waking moment and often affects our ability to rest, relax and sleep.

To deny fear is to refuse to let it go. This rigidity sounds contradictory, but we can only let go of something if we first acknowledge it. If we do not accept it, we are allowing it to be an unwelcome guest in our house and may not even know it is cohabiting with us. On the flip side, once we see and understand the fear and know it, we can begin to release its grip on us. Embrace your feeling and let go. What you resist will persist- as we have all heard many times.

The same can be said for adverse life events. The event is here- resisting will worsen the anguish, letting trauma worm its way into our minds. It is the same as struggling in quicksand. Let go of your obsession with fear. Let go of the fight and accept it as reality.

Everything in life is impermanent, and once we learn to instill this fact in our everyday living, letting go of the past, focusing on the present, and seeing a brighter future -without specific expectations- becomes possible.

Impermanence sounds like "instability" to many people and may be an overwhelming thought. Humans have come to expect to thrive on security and stability, and while we can have that at specific points in our life, nothing is indeed for the long term.

The only stability we can truly rely on is our self-reliance, which can sometimes make us feel as though life is empty: if nothing is permanent and stable, what is the point? The answer is that we learn to appreciate the present, take what we have been given, and do our best with what we have at this moment.

Chodron (1994, pages 23-24) highlights this concept, emphasizing the importance of being able to rely only on the fact that everything changes. We need to stop trying to pin things down and instead allow our perception of the solidity of life to fade away. Every time you come to a solid conclusion, one you believe you can rely on, "let the rug be pulled out from under you" according to Chodron.

This ability to understand impermanence will, in turn, improve your adaptability. We will learn not to be attached to a particular outcome. Instead, get used to change in your everyday life, and eventually, your fundamental pattern of reaction to change will render you more flexible and more resilient. Your brain's ability to rewire itself means it will take on new, more realistic expectations with a relaxed focus, and before you know it, you will find yourself reacting more calmly to the chaotic stresses of life.

Even in the face of life-changing events, your mind, and therefore your body, and emotions, can be prepared for upheaval or change. In "pulling the rug out" from under yourself, Chodron invokes, once again, can lead to the release of expectations of stability, fear, and even of the past.

You may look at life's situational impermanence as permanence in your current reality. Your "truth" could be as simple as seeing your home as a stable base and your job as one you will always love and never lose. While naturally, we can be positive and appreciate what we have right now, Chodron suggests that even these things we should view with a sense of instability and unpredictability. But do not let this perspective incite a sense of fear in you: instead, know that in the present, you have and appreciate these beautiful things in your life, but let go of solidifying and possessing them.

All the passion and emotion you connect with things in your life you can label as "thinking about things" and not fact. This "thinking" provides a means to regulate your emotional over-attachment to specific aspects and objects in your life, allowing the space for a more rational acceptance of events that will become easier to let go of.

As Chodron says, "use the labeling of "thinking" and use it with great gentleness as a way to touch those solid dramas and acknowledge that you just made them all up with this conversation you are having with yourself." Everything in life is the result of perception. Acknowledge this perception, and you are free of it.

Once again, meditation is a great tool to help you let go and relax. Learning to stop struggling against the facts, resisting our feelings, and denying that things are slipping through our fingers is the ultimate power to build resilience against life's traumas.

Further to building awareness of our impermanence in our consciousness, Chodron (1994, pages 117-119) suggests that we accept the end of that moment and welcome the birth of a new one with every exhale. With every breath, a new moment is forged, the old one a mere memory, and every second of the day, we experience change. So bring your awareness to the fact, learn that constancy is false and change is inevitable, and you will become more accepting of disruptions or interferences that show up in life.

Live in the present at each moment. Let go of your pains of the past because they are just a memory. This sensibility will take time and practice, but once you can focus on the here and now, your emotions become more balanced, and the world does not seem so dark.

Step: Exercise 3

Fear is an unavoidable part of life, as we all know. However, the effects of fear do not have to run our lives entirely.

A simple, daily task to help cope with fear that is surprisingly effective is the repetition of an ongoing mantra. This mantra is simply the word TEMPORARY. Let this become your new mantra, too. Breathe the word in as you repeat it, living in the truth of this phrase every day.

All things are temporary, and this is an immutable fact of life. The good things are temporary, and so too, are the "not so good" things.

Triggers are temporary; traumatic events are temporary; fear can also be temporary. All things must end, and the knowledge that whatever you are going through will one day stop bothering you as much as now, that any ongoing events have their end date, can give you the strength to carry on. You can meet nearly any occurrence, stress, traumatic news, or anxiety that may come with the response—whether verbally or non-verbally—"this is temporary. Things will not always be this way."

Some people may struggle with this, especially considering that while events may pass, some pains will remain with us on multiple levels (from emotional and mental to physical) for a long time. This unwelcome thought may be the case which is why I prefer the simplicity of "temporary." There is less resistance from your mind in accepting this word, yet it still holds enough power to alter our emotional response.

The effects of the mantra hold for challenges, difficulties at home, and difficulties at work, and may even help with trouble sleeping. Remember, if you are currently unable to sleep, this is temporary. You will sleep and sleep deeply again! Regarding sleeping specifically, getting lost in a good book or listening to guided imagery helps me relax and quiet my mind enough for sleep—guided imagery can be powerful medicine.

If you find yourself beginning to stress, repeat the mantra "temporary," calmly breathing in and out. You might just be surprised at the grounding effect. The sense of "free falling" fear will begin to wane over time as you remind yourself of the changeable nature of all life.

BUILDING RESILIENCE THROUGH PERSPECTIVE AND GRATITUDE

L etting go of the root causes of fear has provided the foundation for building a new comprehension of resilience. How can we learn to let go? Mindfulness allows us to acknowledge our emotions and the world around us, directing us away from our emotional struggles to a more rational focus on reality. These are the keys to letting go.

From here, we have begun changing our perspective from one of stability to impermanence. Considering life's temporary and ever-changing reality may leave you feeling empty and lost. Gratitude becomes the all-important piece of this puzzle. If you can begin to see life through a deeper perspective and lens of gratitude, you will rediscover meaning with a new sense of resilience.

On that note, let's start with perspective.

Why is Perspective Important?:

Perspective is how we view, understand, and internalize things around us, ultimately affecting our reactions to everyday events. A setback, conflict, or predicament can be damaging and persistent. However, many factors, including your mind frame, will influence your interpretation in various ways. Your frame of mind does not change the facts, but it does affect the life lessons we can take from something negative happening to us and, therefore, our ability to handle circumstances.

Your perspective may seem set in stone, but with the brain's adaptability comes the promise that this perspective is malleable. Think of a strong opinion you have on some situation now. For example, you see the outside world as dangerous, so you prefer the comfort and safety of your own home. I can guarantee that you did not always think this way. Chances are a life event has caused you to make the connection between emotional turmoil and that specific area of your life, which in turn has molded your perception into negativity and hopelessness. Returning to the idea of our ability to guide the mind's pathways as we experience life's hardships, grounding our emotions is possible.

Our mind's eye takes information and instills these influences, ingraining them repeatedly over the years. This patterned behavior gives us order and a sense of comfort and predictability. Whether factual or inaccurate, our perceptions are conclusive, and the patterns are established. However, just as this perception was learned, it can be unlearned.

The concept that perspective can tell many different stories of just one event is typical. For example, a common exploration of how one's viewpoint can alter fact is the analysis of various individuals' memory of a crime scene or the scene of an accident, comparing their understanding of the events which unfolded before them. Depending on the person's historical understanding of the world, from the angle they observed the incident, and any other additional information they may have been exposed to which other witnesses had not, their memory of the event changes the historical fact of what may have actually occurred. (Barbash, 2019.)

There have been experiments that explore the effects of what is known as "weapons focus," too. For example, suppose a weapon is visible during a crime. In that case, witnesses are less likely to remember details of what happened as their fear response prompted them to focus solely on the weapon's danger. Fear quite literally has altered their perception of factual events.

Because their fear has shifted their perspective, their recounting of the incident is more likely to show errors in scenic description and internal biases, which results in many different accounts of the same incident. This varied outcome can occur with almost anything in life: an event that might leave one person traumatized because of their past life experiences can leave another person walking away emotionally unaffected by the scenario.

Our perspective can alter our subjective truth; depending on which paradigm we see the world through, our reactions to perceived trauma can worsen a situation.

You may not have been given a choice of what occurred, but you have a choice in how to view it and respond. The good news is that our perspectives can change. How we decide to view the world is a choice. It may be a choice ingrained into the concept of who we are as a person, and it may be a choice that is difficult to alter, but it is a choice, nonetheless. Knowing that our perspective is a choice, often molded by our past experiences and our understanding of the world as a child, we can learn to identify other ways of dealing with situations, seeing them from a different point of view entirely.

Open your mind, take a step back from your emotions and thoughts and consider how someone else might view your situation. If you struggle to put yourself in the shoes of a conceptual "other person," put yourself in the shoes of someone you already know. Consider how they might view the struggles you are facing.

For example, a failing marriage can lead you to thoughts of despair and hopelessness, projections of your future as a lonely singleton incapable of sustaining a healthy relationship. Someone in your position might see this failing marriage as an opportunity for freedom: freedom from relationship expectations, freedom to live life more independently, and maybe even freedom to find a partner more suited to how you want to live.

The ability to learn and grow from the situation separates the resilient from the vulnerable. It is entirely within your power to turn a perceived negative situation into a positive one and alter your perception at the core of your beliefs, ie "thinking ." Bear in mind, "a belief is just a thought you keep thinking," Esther/Abraham Hicks 2017+- et al. wisely states.

Every situation we find ourselves in has multiple standpoints from which to view it. Seeing these different views may take tremendous energy, particularly if you are in pain. However, once you start to flex your perspective muscles and view an event as a culmination of many characteristics rather than one objective fact, which may be out of your control anyway, you can explore how to turn this event on its head to provide you with a positive outcome.

Admittedly not all perspective shifts will lead to a happy place: some situations in life are so dire and traumatizing that it can be hard to put a positive spin on the experience. Sometimes the only thing to do is bear down in the strength and bravery you are not just processing but developing, seeing obstacles more as challenges we can work through.

Often the negative spiral we find ourselves in is an easy place to remain "stuck in". The news is terrible and extreme. It can take a lot of self-work and self-reflection to begin the first step in tuning out. The ordeals we face can seem impossible to view in a more manageable way.

I promise that with determination, it is entirely possible.

Being stuck in our old negative perspective is habitual. We have learned to see the world one way, and even if that perspective focuses on the negative, we are comfortable with what we know and expect what we expect. So there can be a sense of loss when trying to change our mindset as if we will lose an essential part of ourselves or forget an element of understanding in clinging to this negativity as part of our reality.

Nevertheless, I encourage you to take that leap of faith into the unknown. Consider looking at things from a different paradigm and ease yourself into another dimensional focus. You'll find the benefits you reap much greater than the losses, and a renewed sense of strength will build within you.

We've discussed a little about seeing an end date to the severity of our suffering if we cannot see an upside to the traumatic event itself. There is significant power in imagining the future when our turmoil is over. If we struggle to change our perspective of the present, we often find it easier to alter our perception of the future. We know every single event has an end date, and even though the effect of this event may linger, the pains will diminish over time. We also know that with persistence through adversity, our strength and resilience expand.

This reminder of the future alleviation of our suffering is called positive projection: we are projecting positive outcomes into our future vision. This sense of an end date gives us hope and determination, as we know that if we push through, we will experience a sense of peace again. You can make it, and with a vision of what this "other side" is in mind, you can spur yourself on with a renewed sense of hope.

Lovering (2022) states that imagining future positives is an effective strategy to aid individuals in persisting through hard times. Suppose we change our perspective of the future by imagining positive outcomes. This vision of an unknown future can be considerably easier than changing our view of a problematic present. In that case, we can shape our destinies.

Changing our perception of the future, much like the present, requires focus. This focus can be harnessed through mindfulness, primarily through meditation. Take some time out of your day, even if it's as little as five minutes, to clear your surroundings of distraction and clear your mind of thoughts. While you are at it, remember taking 10-15 minutes during the day to nap to clear your mind can jumpstart not only your energy but the reprogramming of your mind.

Napping is an understated form of medicine. "Sleep is the best meditation," the Dalai Lama states unequivocally. We know high-stress levels exhaust us and your body's call to stop everything and rest is elementary—more on reprogramming in my upcoming book.

As you meditate, you don't have to focus on anything, just your clarity of mind. Perhaps you are suffering from an illness that debilitates you, but you know breakthroughs are imminent. Considerations include new strides in treatment options, incredible medical professionals, and support. To imagine this as a future can be momentary-leave it to drift in and out of your awareness.

In this instance, you can imagine a future involved in all the activities you used to enjoy because now you have found a way to manage your perspective on this illness. Feel how your feet hit the ground as you run; imagine the laughter of your friends and family surrounding you as you once again can leave the house. Feel these sensations as reality while you meditate.

While this way may not scratch the surface for some, a projection of wellness has been proven to improve hour-by-hour suffering significantly. The next minute in your mental healing may become more manageable. Guided imagery is an effective tool towards this end. I cannot recommend Belleruth Naparstek enough. Distinguished in her field of social work, her contributions to patient healing through Guided Imagery have been immense. If you can find her recordings, consider making the investment.

No matter your scenario, there are a plethora of imagined futures that you can bring to mind - futures that have alleviated you of your troubles, futures where you have accepted your pain and are managing to heal from it. If you find imagining scenarios difficult, try translating them into sentences instead, especially if your mind wanders to negative perspectives that don't serve you. In the illness scenario, the facts may be—"the treatment I am going through has been proven highly effective, and if I continue on my treatment plan, I will be another success story."

Again, your perspective in settling into meditation will bring you to a better place.The more time spent in meditation with relaxed focus and acceptance, the more you will find your perspective of current events changing for the better. The more you meditate, the more natural these scenarios will feel. Carry these scenes with you in your waking life, believing that things can become positive in time.

With a shift in perspective comes a better understanding of the impermanence of daily life. We become more aware of the capacity for change and how momentary our present is. All we can know for sure is the present moment; depending on our perspective, this moment is brief and elusive. Thinking about the future, therefore, holds restorative power, fueling our present moment with hope, a sense of control, the knowledge that things must always change, and our ability to strive through tough times is limitless.

Change can be fraught with fear of the unknown but altering our perspective to understand the benefits of change is essential. When we deeply consider how fortunate we are to be here now—not only regarding the incredible advances in medicine and technology but also the pure miracle that we are here, formed a million-to-one—the world is illuminated in our eyes.

Our perspective on reality is not to view the modern world as "Pollyanna" perfect —far from it. Our species continues to encounter unchecked reckless violence and insanity, pandemics, natural disasters, war, and the use of deadly weaponry. However, we have also seen and possibly even witnessed for ourselves the extreme capacity for kindness in each other, the desire for humanity to come to the aid of others and adapt, grow, change, and rebuild.

In the face of so many natural disasters and wars, communities band together time and time again. When we can focus on the beautiful parts of society, the traumatic elements hold less power in our minds.

It is often said to always look for the people helping in times of disaster. There you will always find the good in humanity amplified. In communities bonding together to improve lives after a disaster as one cohesive unit, this is where we witness the ultimate resiliency of our collective selves. No matter where you look or how dire the situation is, humanity can bring out the best of itself. We are more compassionate, braver, and resilient than we give ourselves credit for in day-to-day life. Focus your perspective on these beautiful acts of community and empathy, and the world doesn't seem so dark a place.

We are all familiar with Charles Dickens's famous novel "A Tale of Two Cities." The story aside, the words begin the historical novel with prose on the duality of our lives. Dickens perfectly encapsulates the simple reality of humanity and daily life: that there is beauty to be found even amongst the direst of pain: "It was the best of times, it was the worst of times, it was the age of wisdom, it was the age of foolishness, it was the epoch of belief, it was the epoch of incredulity, it was the season of light, it was the season of darkness, it was the spring of hope."

Our world has always been A Tale of Two Cities if you will. With the invention of instantaneous communication and travel, the world is more and more a global community with the depth and heights of our shared humanity woven inextricably throughout. The concept above shows the contrasts that have built our strength, fueled our creativity and development. Our best defenses and means of growth are knowledge, understanding, and empathy, and our perspective helps us detect these beautiful things in the world around us.

However, conditioned constant over-communication in the form of so much social media (not all of it bad) can invalidate our core- perceptions and fill us with self-doubt. How can we see the reality in front of us in a comprehensive way and appreciate the simple moments when we are partaking of other people's world in display- actual or enhanced- at a constant rate? How can we take the moments for what they are, here and gone, and hold them quietly without recording and showing them to the world? How often during even an hour do we find ourselves narrowly focused on our phones and checking in on others' activities instead of simply being present?

Much of social media is a waste of time. There are positives, don't get me wrong. However, more yearly data shows the damage to self-esteem social media can cause, particularly in children. So why spend your life watching others vying for attention when you can refocus your attention and energy on your core and spirit?

The benefits of social media are obvious. You can make worldwide connections, expand your marketing, educate yourself and follow inspirational figures that can sometimes motivate you in your own life. But many people would argue that the negatives of social media far outweigh the positives, and the benefits we garner from social media can be found elsewhere, too.

So, why is social media so bad for us?

For a start, social media has completely revolutionized the way we communicate with each other, and not always for the better. Electronic communications forever changed how we talk to each other, with everything, real or otherwise, being immediate and all-encompassing, making the banal and non-essential seem essential. Also, social media's "edited" version of life has done away with valuable nuances in natural face-to-face dialogue.

Ironically, social media can make us feel lonely, giving us a reason to question our place or sense of self. When constantly surrounded by images of an amalgam of friends, strangers, and celebrities and their success, it's all too easy to controvert or confuse our core perceptions from positive to negative. Unfortunately, these unclear and ambiguous interactions interrupt and morph our consciousness, and our mental health and self-esteem can be compromised.

As we know, numerous studies indicate that the effect of social media on our mental health is negative (Social Media Victims Law Centre, 2022.) Higher use of social media correlates to a higher risk of depression, low self-esteem, loneliness, and anxiety, with the most affected age group being young teenage girls. There is also a strong likelihood of addiction where social media is involved, believe it or not. It is free and easy to access, available to millions of people worldwide, and provides a constant escape from the realities of life. It has even been suggested that it is more addictive than alcohol and cigarettes, so potent is its power over its users. So it is no surprise that any of us might use social media as a distraction from the day, especially if we are dealing with trauma and difficult circumstances.

When we escape into the depth of social media and its various avenues, we deny the reality of our lives. Following the lives of others can make us feel inadequate in our accomplishments, leading to consuming material from content creators and dismissing our individuality. To be mindful means to live in the present, and living in the present is to be aware of our perspective and grow our gratitude. Living mindfully is made so much easier by the elimination of social media.

Perspective is critical, especially today. Times are changing at a much faster rate than humanity has ever faced. Therefore, we must constantly adjust our ways of thinking, being present in a more empathic way so we communicate better. Removing blocks to mindfulness awareness, such as adjusting our utilization of social media, can open the doorway to gratitude.

The Benefits of Gratitude:

We've spoken a little about gratitude, but let's define it properly before discussing its benefits.

The word gratitude derives from the Latin word for grace (Harvard Health Publishing, 2021,) which promotes a thankful appreciation for things we receive. We are grateful when acknowledging the good things that come about, whether physical gifts, intangible emotions like love and empathy, or even when specific events happen to alter our lives for the better.

Our gratitude presents the flip side of our pains. If we can find gratitude where positivity seems impossible, we can find balance and a sense of purpose. A balanced approach to trials and tribulations can then be a natural progression.

Research has suggested that individuals with a higher sense of gratitude in their day-to-day life are, in general, happier. Nurturing a sense of appreciation for even the small things helps us to conjure more positive emotions and appreciate the good things in our life (Harvard Health Publishing, 2021.) When we notice how much we have to be thankful for, the negativity in our lives doesn't seem as overwhelming. As a result, the scales of life are more balanced.

Search within yourself for things in your life you can be genuinely grateful for, focus your attention on them, and over time you will find the positives of your life weighing out the negatives. This renewed sense of positivity will be another link in your armor against the aggression of life.

It's all too easy for me to sit here and tell you to find gratitude in your life, and things will become a little more manageable. If someone had come to me a mere few years ago and told me the same thing—to find gratitude when my life seemed to be crumbling around me—I'm not sure my reaction would have been very polite.

Finding things to be grateful for, searching for the positive when you struggle to leave your bed in the morning for fear of what the day might hold, is no mean feat. The path to gratitude might be arduous, and baby steps are needed to make your way on that journey. Think of this journey of finding gratitude as if you were making your way up a steep hill. Going straight up is likely not the best path and will leave you exhausted. However, if you traverse the mountain back and forth, this slow and more measured approach will lead you much more effectively to your goal at the top with your wits about you. Ease is what you are looking for. Keeping easy thoughts and lighter feelings of appreciation here or there will take the pressure off of yourself.

A good start is to understand that you're once again not denying the negative by appreciating the positive. Life is full of contrast—it's what makes the world go round, the tides rise and fall and the day bright and the night dark. The distinction of contrast is everywhere you look, and you can be certain your life is no different. A change in perspective means acknowledging the darkness and training yourself to look for the light. We can train ourselves to be grateful for even a glimmer of positivity.

It is always there, waiting to be uncovered, no matter how small.

Contrasts in life are painful. Most of us would rather have positive experiences to deal with and never come across a negative one again. So how do we find gratitude despite often intense contrast? Among the prolific teachings of Abraham Hicks (et al. l +2019), the discourse on the topic of contrast is fundamental. By knowing what you don't want, you know more clearly what you do want. With the experience of darker chapters in our life, we can more fully experience the brighter ones. We need to know what to focus our energy on to achieve our desired life.

Most of us might agree that a life full of positivity and goodness would be far greater than a balanced one. No surprise that we don't thrive in discomfort and would much rather live in a situation where nothing terrible happens to us. Nevertheless, the contrast in life makes us think along these lines in the first place. We yearn for a more pleasant environment entirely because we may have experienced it once, and it has now escaped us. Alternatively, we have never experienced such an environment and yearn for it. We long for love and acceptance simply because we may not have felt it recently and, from past experiences, know the joy and fulfillment it can bring.

One way we can bring more positivity into our lives is to adjust our focus on what we want. We see the negative, accept it, and let it go, realigning our perspective to allow all the positives of life to flow to us. Once we train ourselves to notice the positives, we will view life more and more clearly. As we show gratitude for the greatness life has offered, the more likely we can cope when things go wrong for a while, possibly even attracting more positivity along the way.

Contrast also allows us the opportunity to improve. Imagine a world with no turmoil, no heartbreak, and no strife. On the surface, this sounds perfect—an idyllic place where pain and suffering are no longer. However, it might not be as heavenly as you imagine. With nothing to make us strive for better, imagine how sedentary life would be without inventions or medical advancements. There would be no cause to develop and improve. Empathy, compassion, and love for others would be stifled. On a personal level, why learn and grow if there is nothing for which to learn and grow?

Without the contrast between good and bad, we would be in perpetual limbo with no reason to seek. How can we know what we truly want without the full breadth of human experience to drive our wishes? Just as the good can motivate us to get through difficult times, the bad gives us opportunities for growth and development.

Learn to be grateful for this, and you can take life's lessons more in stride.

As we interact in the world around us, we derive meaning and, most importantly, choose how we focus our awareness. Some people argue that it is entirely our awareness that makes us who we are. To be conscious is to exist; existing is defined only by our consciousness. As Descartes famously said, "I think, therefore I am." Our awareness and what we choose to pay attention to are at the foundation of our lives.

You are more than capable of shifting your awareness and, therefore, your perspective to a brighter one, knowing dire situations will change. You choose how you see the world around you. Furthermore, from Hicks's (2021) teachings, we can learn to be grateful for the act of appreciation itself. Much like how the darkness in life helps us appreciate the brightness, a lack of gratitude can eventually lead us to an abundance of gratitude. How? You may feel a lack of appreciation for your situation right now, but know that this will only serve to brighten even the most superficial sensations of thankfulness in the future. So don't give up the benefit of acknowledging the contrasts in life.

When you find yourself in a state of appreciation no matter how big or small—from being grateful for a promotion at work to appreciating the beautiful colors of a butterfly as it flits past—hold yourself there. Bask in the good feelings and feel more alignment. Appreciation adds more to the value of what already is. During this meditation on gratitude, find in yourself the natural ability to be thankful for what you are receiving. It's natural to feel grateful in your life; furthermore, it's natural to receive good things. The more you revel in those good feelings, the more you can apply them elsewhere in your life as you exercise the muscles of gratitude until they become strong, second nature.

To summarize gratitude concerning perspective, as Esther Hicks perfectly explains, "when you know what you DON'T want, you more clearly know what it is you DO want." So naturally, you realign your focus on what you want from life, and you will see more and more, building a sense of positivity about the world and what it might have in store for you. Then, apply your gratitude in good times and in bad times. Over time, it will be a daily habit, enriching your life without even trying. With this gratitude, we can change our perspective by being grateful for whatever eventually arises out of adversity, which can change our outlook on our life.

Personal Note:

I, for one, certainly know the difficulties of applying gratitude to extremely tough situations. A few years ago, my health unexpectedly declined to a point where I had to endure a month-long stay in the hospital, fighting for my life and uncertain of any future. Things were not looking good- that is putting it mildly.

Due to my health condition, my blood had to be drawn and tested every few hours. Whatever precious moment I dozed off after hours of trying to sleep in total agony, I would be awoken yet again by a nurse ready with a needle to check me. My suffering was unimaginable, and there were times when the pain and exhaustion were so intense that I struggled through with silent tears in isolation, struggling to even concentrate on my own thoughts. Even then, though, I could find a morsel of fortitude. As a man down the hall wailed and moaned all night long, I conjured the gratitude to think, "there's no guarantee that this man is in more pain than me... and yet here I am, harboring the force not to cry out and cope with my strife in a quieter, more measured manner." Either way, no matter the outcome, I knew things would not always be this way. I accepted the future for better or worse because, right at that moment, I was determined. It was not my time to give up.

We all deal with pain differently, of course. Still, at that time, I found a means to improve my perception of the situation while also congratulating myself on a strength I previously hadn't acknowledged. I knew I would get through that difficult time and will continue to do so because I have my core—my spirit—in this material world and the next. So please find it in yourself to truly appreciate your independence and grace.

Perception is the difference between life and death, hope and despair. With practice, we can refocus our perception on the positives of ourselves, the world around us, and even situations plaguing us. Newfound gratitude will creep its way into your mind, and more and more, you will see beauty in the world around you. Let this beauty stir in your heart and guide you to a more peaceful, calm present. You are well on your way to being that resilient person.

Step: Exercise 4

Here we are, exercise four, which focuses on applying perspective and gratitude in your life and noticing its positive effects daily.

You might be surprised to learn that, at first, you don't necessarily need to drastically change how you live to experience the positives of life. All you need to do is do a little digging, search for them, find what already exists in your world and acknowledge it. But, most importantly, take a moment to congratulate yourself for getting this far!

This step is two-fold- easy and doubly effective.

You may not be a social media lover, but if you are, reducing or even stopping your time spent watching the lives and opinions of strangers is a decisive step. Not only will you gain a more grounded sense of yourself, but you can learn the benefits of simplicity. Your reality will be less focused on comparison to others and where it could be focused- on your newfound clarity of mind.

So consider your relationship with social media. Start with one crucial step: turn off social media of any kind— no Instagram, no Twitter, no Facebook—just for one day. See how you fare. You might find it surprisingly tricky as you're used to constantly checking in on events and other people's lives. You may begin to feel like you're missing out. You may feel a little urge to turn your socials back on but resist. For just one day, see how things go. Notice how much more present and aware you become and how the lack of constant comparison affects your mood and perspective. I believe after a few days you won't miss it. Your eyes may be more open to your surroundings and possibly how you can improve said surroundings.

If you're just an occasional social media user, that's great. Now let's see if you can take down your usage time even further, using social media for only "essential" reasons - promoting your business, or being part of a support group, for example.

You will be surprised at how little you use the information you find through endless posting from other people and endless scrolling through their feeds. Very little of this information will benefit your day-to-day life, so take what you need and leave the rest behind. Eventually, you will realize that social media hinders your personal growth and mental health.

If you manage one day free of social media, try another. Keep pushing yourself to stay away. You will realize that this new perspective on life's positives is about simply letting the beneficial aspects of life affect you.

So instead of reaching for the daily feed, you can now feed your soul by taking that moment to acknowledge and appreciate what you have- no matter what it is.

You've no doubt been through some turbulent times. I can bet that there were times you were a breadth away from giving up. Regardless, you have reached the other side; you've made it. You are here. Appreciate your current self for your courage even in witnessing adverse situations, and you will find a renewed appreciation for your power. Rest assured, it is there!

Collect your ideas. Use your phone for jotting these things down, or start collecting on pieces of paper or a notebook.

Write down something you can feel solidly grateful for. Maybe you are thankful for a slight improvement in your or your loved one's health today; you are just happy it isn't raining, or you're grateful for that delicious cup of coffee this morning. You are surrounded by things to be thankful for, even as you experience challenges. Maybe only some things are perfect now but think of it like a radio, receiving loads of signals, but you're tuned in to an unclear frequency. By re-tuning, and recalibrating, you will find a better signal where the clear sound comes through. Noticing even the most simple things is like this. You are tuning in. The more you acknowledge, notice and appreciate, the more gratitude builds, and you will see more positives in your life.

If you find it challenging to think of anything, just write when you notice a moment of feeling grateful. The simple act of writing things down solidifies them as positives, so catch yourself thinking good things. Collecting and reading over everything you have expressed thanks for is a productive activity when the mood strikes. Bask in the lightness and in that headspace for as long or as short a time that feels right. Your reality will be less focused on comparison to others and where it should be, on your newfound perspective, clarity of mind, and your grace.

MAINTAINING RESILIENCE

You've got the steps and foundation to building resilience through determination and a mindset change. Once you've put them into practice, you'll be well on your way to developing your fortitude in times of adversity, but that's only half the battle. True resilience lies in the ability to maintain it.

Maintaining resilience relies upon empathy, clear communication, and inserting yourself into the "shared experience" of difficult times and emotions. Through having suffered the lows of life, our ability to empathize increases. With this empathy comes the ability to calmly and effectively communicate with the world around us.

Our knowledge of our shared experience can enhance our composed response in times of crisis. Therefore, we can effectively diffuse the emotion of the moment, take the temperature down, and show those around us how to handle, respond to, and manage a trying time.

In this chapter, you will see that with our empathic ability, our "leadership" role in times of distress naturally occurs. This concept of resilience is circular, really. Knowledge and power lead to empathy, self-control, guidance, and leading by example, which in turn leads to an increase in your ability to bounce back all over again. Tap into this cycle, and witness the positive effects on your life and those around you.

Now that you have found a way to build gratitude and grace no matter your situation, have acknowledged your core strength and spirit, and know you can rely on your bravery and resilience, the next step in your journey is to focus on those around you.

The Importance of Empathy:

Empathy is an emotional response you're sure to know and have experienced. It is the emotion of being able to identify with the feelings of other people, see things from their perspective, assess the potential reasons for why someone is expressing the feelings they're experiencing, and the ability to be affected and share the emotional state of another without experiencing the trauma (directly) (De Waal, 2009.).

So powerful is this innate human ability to empathize; this emotion extends further beyond our own species. We experience empathy for animals, the environment, and each other without even trying. This evolutionary trait benefits our communities and the world as a whole.

According to De Waal (2009), empathy consists of two components. The first is cognitive, relating to how we think about the situation of another, how we imagine ourselves in their shoes, recalling our past experiences and memories to make sense of their plight or issue. Because this side of empathy requires a high level of cognition and language, this is often categorized as a purely human trait. Our ability to think through situations abstractly and apply our own understanding of the pains of others is seen only in human thinking (as far as we are aware).

However, this component of empathy doesn't demonstrate the depth and breadth of compassion seen in the natural world. Infants and young children can show and feel empathy even though their cognitive abilities are not fully mature and their language skills are underdeveloped. This response suggests there is a more intangible component to empathy, one that cannot be measured in intelligence but in pure emotion. This pure emotional connection requires no thinking or abstract thought to place ourselves in the relative sense of another's situation. Instead, this side is pure instinct, our natural ability to sense the mood and stresses of those around us. Many animals, even with low cognition, are capable of showing signs of empathy, suggesting that its evolutionary and survival benefits are multiple and universal.

We can think empathetically; we can emote empathy; our body can sense the need for compassion from the emotional state of others. Without this sensitive, caring side, no amount of thinking and imagining of another's pain will invest you in understanding their suffering to the same level. De Waal (2009) believes that even if you can understand the other's perspective, genuine empathy cannot be achieved without emotional investment.

We can share experiences on many levels. When we can empathize with others, remember that they can empathize with us, too. So in that sense, at least, you are never alone.

Seeing others who have been through similar experiences aids in our understanding of human resilience and strength. Witnessing those who have suffered and bounced back from adversity fosters perspective within yourself. Your flexibility in times of trouble can naturally reverberate in peaceful responsiveness- even buoyancy- in times of crisis. As a situation unfolds in front of you, you are able to take a leadership role reflective of those around you, further augmenting your consistent ability to rely on your strength in future events or times of upheaval.

In times of pain, find it within yourself to tap into your empathy and the power that ensues. Find that unanticipated calm leader that has always been inside you and uncover the potential it holds. There is comfort in the knowledge that others understand what we're feeling, what we're going through, and vice versa. So we have the ability to share this comfort just as we receive it.

Some examples of the most famous figures enduring hardships with insight that ultimately benefited their community on a broader scale are Mother Teresa and Nelson Mandela.

As a child Mother Teresa strongly felt the call of God, dedicating her life to a nunnery at the mere age of eighteen. She was sent to India to teach. Seeing the suffering, poverty, and pain surrounding her daily, she decided that more needed to be done for the world's people.

Already having sacrificed her life to the devotion of God, Mother Teresa decided she needed to give more still, setting up a congregation that cared for those forgotten, such as individuals dying of leprosy, HIV and AIDs, and tuberculosis. She educated the poorest and set up numerous facilities to improve the lives of those around her; soup kitchens, dispensaries, mobile clinics, orphanages, and counseling programs. With her only natural resource being her tenacity, strength, and resilience, Mother Teresa gave her all to the lives of others worldwide.

Nelson Mandela is another globally famous name for bravely championing others after enduring adversity. Born to the Madiba clan in Africa, Mandela faced trials and tribulations early on in his life. The first was his father's death when he was just twelve years old, promoting the young Mandela to the ward of his father's people. He experienced his people's struggles and vowed to fight for their freedom. A young Mandela was expelled from university for joining a student protest, a precursor to the years of punishment and imprisonment ahead of him.

Mandela's activist protests culminated in being sentenced to death in what became known as the Rivonia Trial, a trial in which he vowed in one of his most revered speeches:

"I have fought against white domination, and I have fought against black domination. I have cherished the ideal of a democratic and free society where all persons live together in harmony and with equal opportunities. It is an ideal which I hope to live for and to achieve. But if need be, it is an ideal for which I am prepared to die." (Speech from the Dock quoted by Nelson Mandela on 20th April 1964.)

Despite the multitude of challenges and struggles along Mandela's way, he was eventually freed from imprisonment and inaugurated as South Africa's first-ever democratically elected President. This honor was a role he took seriously and committed himself to unite people.

Even after his leadership ended, Mandela set up multiple charities and foundations as a means to continue his humanitarian work, never wavering in his devotion to equality, democracy, and justice.

As we can see in these two examples of benevolence and empathy in the face of challenges, Mother Teresa and Nelson Mandela's journeys were interwoven with tales of their own suffering, hardship, and upheaval. Despite this (or possibly even because of this) both Mother Teresa and Nelson Mandela were able to channel their painful beginnings into meaningful action and justice. Their experience of sharing with others their understanding of suffering and curating their struggles would continue to benefit people the world over for generations to come.

To channel our pain to benefit our lives and the lives of others, even in more minor everyday ways, we must first start where we are.

Through our own losses and strife, we relate to the losses and strife of others. Chodron (1994, pages 67-68) tells of this sense of our renewed enlightenment of others due to our own experiences. As a result of our struggles, our understanding of empathy is heightened. As a result of what we might have been through, it occurs to us that we can feel empathy.

This connection to the rest of humanity can lead to a profound experience where we can feel the weight of those struggling around us, and we realize that although our suffering is personal, it is always, in some way, a universal experience. Empathizing with the struggles of others will not always mend our situations, but it opens our hearts and soul to people with whom we previously would not have had a sense of shared experience.

Chodron continues by emphasizing this shared struggle of humanity, stating that we are the latest in a long line of people who have survived the ages due to our innate, profound ability to feel and recognize our commonalities and fates. As a "neighbor in empathy," any one of us can have an understanding among family and friends, even strangers. As Pema Chodron eloquently says, "This is where the sense of gratitude and appreciation for our life comes from. We become part of a lineage of people who have cultivated their bravery throughout history, people who, against enormous odds, have stayed open to great difficulties and painful situations and transformed them into the path of awakening. We will fall flat on our faces again and again, we will continue to feel inadequate, and we can use these experiences to wake up, just as they did.....a means to connect with the power of our lineage, the lineage of gentle warriorship." By being simply a pillar of empathy and understanding to our family and friends, there is no doubt that we are subjects within this "lineage of gentle warriorship."

Think on this long line of those before us. How did we get to where we are now? How did these medical advancements come about, and how did we find the ability to improve scientific study and sociological understanding? Through empathy. Empathy expands the human race in the best of ways.

Generation after generation, the human race has faced dangers, fears, and obstacles of varying severity, sometimes in passionate resolve. As a result, we have thrived. The obstacles and pain we face are this shared lineage, whether through our ancestors experiencing the exact same scenarios or experiencing the same emotions and sense of threat. Though times have changed, our connection to our resilient heritage remains. With the suffering and consequent resolve and resilience of our ancestors, we have come to be where we are today. Though we may not be fighting the same war, we are gentle warriors, like our ancestors before us, in the battle against fear, anxiety, and strife.

We have the ability to continue this gentle warriorship in standing with our brothers and sisters in times of trouble. Do not close yourself off from the world around you. Share your struggles and empathy, and you will receive the same in return.

Emotional Reciprocity:

Multiple studies over the last few decades exemplify the benefits of the shared human experience. As these experiences are amplified, so too are they improved.

Reciprocity means to exchange something for mutual benefit. Emotional reciprocity, therefore, refers to the mutual benefit we as humans experience when we share our emotions, experiences, and struggles.

On a basic level, studies suggest that humans are wired for emotional reciprocity, with an automatic tendency to mimic the non-verbal actions, reactions, and emotional expressions of others when talking to them (Perakyla and Stevanovic, 2015.) This natural copying is said to affect the emotions of the person being subconsciously copied:

they are more likely to feel heard and understood, as if they are not alone in their experiences. This reflection happens without our knowledge, as it is not a cognitive response but an innate need for connection and emotional intimacy.

Human beings are therefore driven to share our experiences, especially if we share an environment, in search of this mutual understanding and sense of companionship. If you share your experiences, you will notice this emotional reciprocity all around you. People will empathize, mimic your emotions and behaviors in an unconscious attempt to soothe your pains, and just as others do this for you, so do you do this for others. If you try to help others, your sense of community and emotional connection will only serve to strengthen your resolve and hope in your own struggles and strife.

The demonstration of empathy in times of turmoil is the demonstration of your innate human nature. You don't have to understand what someone is going through ultimately, nor do you have to agree with their point of view. Instead, empathy is seeking to improve your understanding of someone else's pain and to help them feel understood (Baker, 2016.)

Empathy builds trust, helps us communicate more effectively, and influences and resolves conflict, but it is an arguably underused skill in many of us today. Break that pattern. Utilize the power of empathy to improve the lives of those around you and your own. Connect to the world around you, see things from different points of view now and then, and your sense of self will become indestructible over time.

The ability to feel for others even when coping with your issues shows the greatest strength of character. This strength of character displays empathy, which can unite us and relieve the weight of our burdens.

The Importance and Benefits of Leading by Example:

So, we know some of the benefits of showing empathy and seeking out situations where we can share this empathy and improve our lives in the process. From here, I encourage you to be open to the idea of leading by example.

Effective, empathetic, and calm communication will help you deal with authority in times of crisis. Empathy will guide you and your team on the way to success if you're amongst a group of people. Hawthorne and Lowenbraun (2022) state that the best communicators in business scenarios perfectly balance their authority with a sense of empathy. Not only do people trust those with authority, but they feel secure and understood when their leader emotes empathy, resulting in team members being more likely to trust their boss and follow through with actions that will benefit the whole team. In fact, studies have concluded that employees value high levels of emotional intelligence and empathy among good communication and people management skills, as the most critical interpersonal skills for leadership, above more nuanced and tangible skills such as financial management and data analysis (Poulsen, 2022.) People are more likely to trust and respond to those they believe will listen to and empathize with them. Would you rather have a boss who knows all the statistics and analytical aspects of their company but has poor communication skills, or a boss who is willing to hear your problems, talk them through to a mutually beneficial solution, and display leadership in understanding and empathy when things get hard? I know which one I would choose.

Robust and empathetic communication can be an especially relevant skill in times of crisis. Good communication is essential in achieving resolution after a conflict or disaster. Empathy allows us to comfort those in pain and strife, ensuring you build a sense of trust with others to pull together more effectively. Without compassion, poor communication is inevitable, which can exacerbate panic and a lack of confidence.

To bring this leadership quality into your own life is to trust yourself. Building your self-esteem and self-realization and helping others around you is a direct result of your use of empathy. Most people learn by example. Focus on goodwill, do what's within your limits for those around you, and lend a listening ear and an open heart even in challenging situations. Practice the empathy you preach and watch your support network grow.

When I speak of leading by example, I do not just mean in times of crisis. Some of the most successful teachers, particularly of youth and young adults, are empathetic communicators. If we build our children with a sense of security and understanding, the likelihood that they will pass this skill on to their peers and their children is tenfold. Creating a more supportive and stable society begins with any one of us.

Teach others the art of empathetic communication by practicing this skill yourself. There's no pressure here, as it's the practice itself. So when someone is talking to you, truly listen to what they are saying, engage with their words and meaning. Ask questions, and be curious about who this person is -even if you may not be friends or have much in common. Practice patience, especially if the person you're talking to is experiencing a particularly stressful time. Simply bring more awareness to your interactions with people and see if you can practice empathy at that moment. You never know what you will learn from genuinely connecting with those around you, and the stories of others might inspire strength in your own.

You can give back to the world by maintaining resilience once you've built strength within yourself. It is a resolve to remain here within this legacy of problem solvers. You have been through trials and tribulations, and you can help build strength in others by example. Share your stories and knowledge with empathy, knowing that you will be in a better place as you give to the world. Nurture this resiliency in others, and feel it grow more robust in you.

This simple idea is the final "step" in your journey of strength and resilience. You remain in this place of resolve and radiate a peaceful state of being, a knowingness that those around you will see and feel. You won't even have to try. There is no "convincing" anyone. You have been through it; you understand it so deeply. This resilient person is now who you are.

Confidence is found in facing the immutable fact that life is ever-changing and ever evolving. What might be considered a "major setback" or upheaval may appear daunting initially; however, the softness and calmness in meeting it here will radiate to those around you. The people in your environment benefit from the energy in your composure. You have completed the cycle. You are now a part of this "lineage of gentle warriorship." Thank you, Pema Chodron, for this lovely truth.

There is no more to this last step. Just think of this eloquent reference to resilience and being part of this ever-evolving, ever-growing" lineage of gentle warriorship," and you are there.

BONUS CHAPTER
ONGOING STABILITY, RESILIENCY AND HEALTH

W elcome to the final chapter- Chapter Six- a bonus chapter with simple ideas for ongoing stability, resilience, and a healthy you. You know you can effectively manage setbacks and face crises by carefully controlling your emotions, and you can carry this ability throughout your life. The knowledge and five essential skills you have learned in the previous five chapters have set the foundation for resiliency. Resiliency will improve your health, and your health will improve your resilience.

Keep this book handy, and refer to this chapter time and again for easy real-life reminders.

Many of these tips may seem insignificant, but they play an integral role in this concept of steadfast resilience.

These ideas will support ongoing management regarding your home, health, and mental well-being. Focus on your strength and improve your health and fortitude as you move forward on your journey.

The fundamentals rely on the intangibles, the mental and the metaphysical- your core, spiritual and emotional health. Secondly, we cannot deny how the physical – your surroundings, your environment, if simplified and functioning as they should, enhance your ability to perform better.

Let's focus on your core.

Your Metaphysical Life

How do you keep on top of your mental and emotional life? By maintaining control.

We know how to become more resilient and better look after our mind and body to cultivate a perfect environment for resilience to blossom. But how do we maintain this environment? Let's cover some basics.

This book provides tried and true techniques for increasing resilience and improving your mental health and well-being. The following suggestions focus more on soundness, stability, and nourishing positivity.

Self-Kindness:

Practice self-kindness daily. The effect of self-kindness is not just to enhance your confidence. A second effect is to stop and slow your "monkey mind"- or negative feedback loop, reminding yourself to take care of what is important- your mental health. A mantra is a great way to remind yourself.

Mantra:

Whether your mantra continues to be "TEMPORARY," as suggested in step 3 or not, a personal mantra posted on your desk or where you will see it daily is an indispensable ingredient for potency and confidence.

Choose one or more positive messages to yourself. You can even positively address negative physical traits. Traits you may wrongly believe to be true can be a good start. We all wrestle with insecurity at various times in our lives; this may be an excellent time to address this. Mantras should be brief lists to boost ideas like self-respect, confidence, understanding, and receptivity to change. They work well if they make a repetitive sound which can aid concentration in meditation. For example, say your mantra to relax, begin your meditation, or just read it while walking by or sitting at your desk. Make communicating your mantra part of your routine.

Vision:

If you decide to continue your daily five-minute medi-
tations as suggested in earlier chapters, you're on to an
excellent start. To expand on this practice, spend
another five minutes in the meditative position -
sitting or lying down- repeating affirmations that mean
something to you. Try to come up with your own –
while you can certainly take inspiration from asser-
tions you already know, conjuring your own will speak
more directly to your sense of self, impacting your
mindset.

Some simple affirmations to reinforce belief in yourself
include:

- I am patient with myself.
- I accept myself, my flaws, and my strengths.
- I can achieve what I set my mind to.
- I am mentally strong and getting stronger
  every day.

Use these as inspiration and tailor your imagery
accordingly.

Tailoring your imagery, even more specifically, is something you can do on the front cover of your journal if you
keep one. Using this cover as your vision board is a
straightforward simple and confidential means of

expanding your mind and looking forward to a hopeful future or change.

To create this vision cover, consider your dream job, your dream house, your dream partner, future successes, and anything you can imagine creating for yourself. Once you have the ideas in mind, search online or in magazines for images that represent these hopes. Collect them and assemble a grouping of them on your journal. This cover is easy to keep private, so no one even flippantly discredits what you see for yourself. This cover is an excellent motivator for not getting distracted or discouraged. With this daily reminder of what you aim for, you can work towards your future more clearly.

Maintaining your choices guilt-free:

Another vital factor to begin implementing in your life is your ability to say no. Many of us are people pleasers, which can lead to us doing tasks we don't necessarily want to or feel comfortable doing. It is okay to express when you do not have the emotional or physical energy right at the minute someone requests something of you. It's easy to burn yourself out with the activities in your own life. The possibility of burnout or resentment becomes very real when taking on too much for others.

It's great to be able to help where you can but remember to factor in your own needs first, which will give you more room to accommodate others. The more you practice this, the less guilt you will feel. You must be your number one supporter.

Agency:

Agency is crucial in maintaining control over what is in our grasp. Agency refers to our capacity to act according to our observations, not letting life wash over us passively. Without agency, a sense of hopelessness, despair, and lack of control can take over our lives.

We can improve our sense of agency in many ways.

The first means of improving our agency is practicing our ability to control stimuli's power to affect us. Nothing from our outside world can creep into our internal perceptions unless we let it. Agency is a concept we are familiar with from learning about the realignment from the negative to the positive.

At times, selectively choosing our focus can be difficult. Napper and Rio (2019) suggest that if our environment overwhelms us and we cannot escape external pressures forcing their way into our minds, our best bet is to practice going quiet, as we have discussed with mindfulness and meditation, and planting ourselves in screen-free environments, especially if you're prone to "doom-scrolling" (which is the act of spending excessive amounts of time reading and absorbing negative news) on your phone or laptop.

Restoration:

The most restorative environments are convening in nature, whether a stroll along a winding river, getting lost in a woodland, or a village walk for fresh air. It also helps to turn off your notifications when you're trying to concentrate or need a bit of space and to isolate yourself from hectic and noisy social situations for a little while. Doing these things enables you to regain a sense of control, calming your mind and easing your racing thoughts until you feel ready to face the world again. You are effectively controlling stimuli, returning to your core.

Controlling stimuli also refers to controlling the type of people we choose to surround ourselves with. It is near impossible as humans to remain unaffected by the people around us. Whether they are close friends and family, acquaintances, or mere strangers, the emotions, attitudes, and behaviors of those we surround ourselves with can significantly impact our feelings, attitudes, and behaviors.

For instance, have you ever been in a great mood entering work, only to find your joy dampened as the day progressed because everyone else seemed to be down? Or maybe you were feeling bummed, but after a visit from a good, cheerful friend, you find your mood elevated, and things don't seem so bad anymore? These are just small examples of how people can affect your daily life. This is where selective association comes into play.

Selective Association:

Where possible, set boundaries for the people you want in your life. Disassociate from negative or pessimistic people, say "yes" when you mean yes and "no" when you mean no, and refuse to let anyone sway your moral, emotional, and physical boundaries when you feel uncomfortable or unsafe. Sometimes, these people and situations are unavoidable, especially in a workplace environment. In this case, learn to emotionally disengage from those who only serve to grind you down.

If members of your family zap your energy or are rigid in their agendas, it is okay to step back. Often the stress of someone else's expectations leads to unnecessary complications. It is usually simpler to keep distance and space to avoid misunderstandings. Remember, saying no is not just a negative- handled gently but firmly-particularly in family dynamics- can go a long way to keeping the peace.

Become aware of how your consciousness is subject to the group mindset and peer pressure, figuring out your ethical code without the pressure to conform to people whose opinions you may disagree with.

Instead, surround yourself with people you love and those who feel the same about you. These people can be friends, family, support groups, and entire communities built around supporting and uplifting each other, ensuring each of you meets your fullest potential in every possible way. Find people who will nurture your talents and emotional intelligence and those you feel comfortable doing the same for.

Napper and Rio (2019) state that "these positive social interactions will improve your state of mind and physical health." With these two fundamental components of life strengthened, your sense of control over your life will only reinforce your perseverance and resiliency.

Other ways of increasing your agency, restoration and controlling stimuli include readiness to learn in new situations, managing your emotions (as discussed in previous chapters), and an awareness of how these emotions influence your thought patterns, behaviors, and judgment of situations.

Once you have systems in place to allow yourself to become more in tune with these aspects of your life, you will find yourself trusting your intuition more and more.

Intuition:

Intuition is our gut feeling, a deep inner knowledge of what we want from life, what is best for us, and how we can protect ourselves. This intuition results from our brain collecting data over the years and observing patterns in situations that allow us to predict what might happen in the future and protect us accordingly.

At the start of this process, fear and doubt may have invalidated your sense of intuition to a point where you could not trust it. Anxiety and trauma can override your instincts. However, your intuition is a natural progression of mindfulness practice. In letting go, your mind will be open to what is, and you will be naturally tuned in.

If your intuition tells you not to do something, then don't do it. If your intuition tells you that a person or situation is dangerous, then remove yourself from that person or situation. This instinct is not the same as fear ruling your life. Once you can think with emotional non-responsiveness, you can use the sense of distress to push you forward. Intuition feels your unease and tells you whether to act or not.

When we use our intuition wisely, our sense of agency increases. We can make decisions based solely on how we think and feel without external input taking control of our lives.

Napper and Rio (2019) continue by stating that in situations involving "unclear social demands with few rules to navigate them," intuition paves the way for us to act according to what we feel is appropriate. Once you can garner more information about your surroundings and social situations, you can change your approach accordingly.

Learn to label your thoughts and feelings with a quiet mind. With a healthy mindset, your intuition will guide you on the right path to self-realization, confidence, and agency.

Your Physical Self and Surroundings

Let's reinforce how physical health and environment bolster your frame of mind even further.

In a depressive or anxious episode or amid turmoil, physical health is often the last thing on your mind. You might find you barely have the energy to get out of bed, let alone clean, exercise or cook. In times of struggle, you may find the call of sugary comfort foods even more alluring. These urges are all perfectly normal, but the positive difference you will see in yourself if you are determined to eat healthily and take charge of your environment will be undeniable. There are a few simple things you can do to take control immediately.

The most simple and effective way to make a change right at this moment in your physical life is through organization. Organization in your physical space positively influences your headspace, allowing you to focus on yourself and loved ones, not your mess.

Life is busy, and your home and work environment can quickly suffer due to your divided attention and the constant speed of life. Without staying on top of your household tasks, they can pile up, creating disorganization in your home that may contribute to a more disorderly mind. If you're anything like me, you'll find your thoughts have more clarity, and you are less stressed if your environment is clear, too.

My first recommendation to improve your physical world is to start with your immediate surroundings. The first instance you have some free time, even a free ten minutes, get to work reorganizing your space. To start, sort through everything you have at your disposal, and anything you don't want or that no longer serves you, throw it on the floor. You can then bin it, recycle it, donate it to charity or pitch it out. The choice is yours, but regardless, if you don't find a use for it, don't keep it hanging around.

Organization can trickle down even into the minutiae of your life. If you're struggling with organizing on a large scale, why not start with a smaller problem area? Look in that one household drawer that keeps a variety of miscellaneous stuff and sort through that. A clean drawer like this may seem insignificant, but a little can go a long way.

If you sit at a desk all day, start with this area instead. Take time to throw away any old notes and messages, place all your stationery in its rightful place, and delve into your email folder to get rid of junk mail. You might find a benefit in sorting your emails into categories.

Once these smaller spaces are more organized, move on to the entrance of your home, a hallway, or a mudroom. The first place you see when you walk into your home should be clear of clutter, a space that is easy to enter and one that you feel relaxed in, a space in which you can feel yourself begin to settle after time out of the house. Take the time to do this, putting away items unused or no longer in season, creating a welcoming environment that draws you in. I cannot tell you how many people I have helped over the years start a "catch-all" for an entrance. It truly makes all the difference to your mood at home if you're greeted with a tidy, organized space.

The next piece of advice when changing your physical world to improve your life revolves around preparation.

Prepare:

If we prepare, we are more likely to be ready for anything that life throws at us, physically fortified by our ability to arrange everything in order before things go awry.

The best way to prepare is to make sure you have a file on hand full of your important documents, papers, and any other components of your life and that of your family in the event of an emergency. These files can include birth certificates, passports, medical documents, and any legal documents you may have accrued over the years. This form of physical organization will help you in quiet times and dramatically helps in times of crisis. For example, if you need to abandon your home during an emergency or natural disaster or need your medical history in hand as quickly as possible, you can feel reassured that your critical information is ready.

Of course, you can "prepare" for any number of events if that's your thing. Maybe you are anxious about the sociological and natural disasters that leave you and your family in limbo. In this case, you can ease this anxiety by keeping your garage or your basement organized and equipped.

Fill your shelves with first aid equipment, blankets, canned goods, and clean water. Personally, I feel a well-stocked kitchen is enough to ease worries, along with a "let the world be what it will be" mindset! These simple basics may provide the "quick fix" style of peace of mind.

Peace of Mind- Humor:

A sense of humor is another excellent way of maintaining your mind, body, and soul. If you can laugh somehow every day, you will feel your body, thoughts, and troubles become lighter. If anything, you can laugh at the absolute absurdity that is life!

On this note, reading or watching something funny before bed is essential. This time will allow your brain to shut down, distracting it from any of the more intense thoughts you might have been having during the day. You will find you sleep better.

Sleep:

As we all know, adequate sleep is critical to maintaining overall health. Try to set up an infallible sleep routine that lets your body know you're getting ready for bed. Whatever you do to get ready for sleep, make sure these are the last things you do with your day. Don't do these activities and then get back to work of any kind, and certainly don't get lost in your phone screen as you lie in bed. If sleep evades you for a night or two, you will, of course, feel exhausted. Remember the "Temporary" mantra. If sleep deprivation becomes chronic, therapies such as hypnosis and other behavioral therapies can help. The most natural "treatments" are as simple as avoiding caffeine and chronic worry about falling asleep.

Physical Health:

When in a depressive episode or during turmoil, physical health is often the last thing on your mind. You might find you have barely any energy to get out of bed, let alone do some cardio, and any food you can be bothered to make is the easy stuff, like microwave meals. In times of struggle, you may find the call of sweet, sugary foods even more alluring. This is all perfectly normal, but the positive difference you will see in yourself if you are determined to move and eat healthily will be undeniable.

Physical movement improves our circulation, providing our muscles, organs, and brain with the oxygen we need to live our lives. Research has shown that long hours of sitting can be dangerous for your health (Napper, Rio, 2019,) and that movement of any form can reduce the health issues you're susceptible to from sitting down all day. If you have an office job, make sure to stand up from your chair every hour, do a couple of stretches, and go for a little walk (if your job allows it) to get your blood pumping and muscles working once again. Even this tiny amount of exercise can work wonders for your physical and mental health.

Even in your free time, vigorous exercise is optional. While cardio is advised, if you're currently not too fitness oriented, then the thought of jumping straight to intense exercise can be a daunting one. Start with simple movements – maybe watch a Pilates video or walk around your neighborhood once a day. This movement will awaken your body and mind in a way that remaining sedentary will not, and it doesn't have to be complicated or strenuous!

Sitting absorbed in your work or a project can quickly become overwhelming. Assess your mood regularly throughout the day, and if you find your concentration or focus diminishing, get up and move. Remind yourself of your agency by using your body freely and with gratitude, no matter what movements you decide to perform.

Intertwined with the benefits of physical movement come the benefits of eating a healthy diet or at the very least becoming more aware of what we are putting into our bodies.

Simple diet reminders:

One of the most critical diet tips is cutting out most refined sugar. Refined sugar is sugar that does not occur naturally in food (like fruit) and has instead been processed as an ingredient to improve the taste of much of what we eat. There really isn't any benefit to it. Cutting out refined sugar doesn't sound too complex, but it can be no easy feat. In fact, studies suggest that we can become addicted to sugar much in the same way we become addicted to cigarettes and some drugs (Santos-Longhurst, 2020) – sugar targets the same area of the brain that leads to nicotine addiction.

At first, you may experience withdrawal symptoms such as craving sugar more, feeling light-headed, and in some cases, feeling fatigued. Push through these withdrawal symptoms, and see what results await you when you get to the other side. Sometimes we rely too much on the immediate dopamine hit of sugar and not enough on the more balanced mood a balanced diet can bring. This advice is not intended to tell you to cut these lovely things from your life completely. Anything can be eaten in moderation. Just make sure to cut down if you think you're ingesting too much refined sugar. You will know when taking note of your sluggishness or feelings of slight depression after a "sugar high" wears off. We all know what this feels like.

There are little things you can do to cut down on your sugar intake, things that shouldn't impact your life in too bold a manner. For example, put less sugar in your tea and coffee, avoid those massive, caffeinated syrup-infused coffees, switch your high-sugar cereal for unsweetened cereal and add flavor with fruits and berries. You don't have to rearrange your life to feel the benefits of a lower sugar intake.

If you enjoy a cocktail, remember that many of these appealing new combinations contain syrups which, in tandem with alcohol, is a double whammy of sugar for your body to process. Natural citrus and natural sweeteners can be the best options.

The final adjustment I cannot recommend enough is making sure to have olive oil in your daily diet. This sounds simple enough because it is. Every time you need to fry, bake or saute, switch out whatever oil you use for olive oil. The best is the extra virgin olive oil, which retains the most nutrients from the olives. This is an easy alteration to make, and the list of benefits is astounding.

Olive oil is a wonderous oil that has been used across the Mediterranean for centuries. Several studies demonstrate that olive oil reduces the risk of strokes, improves heart health through lowering blood pressure and improving the function of blood vessels, and can reduce the risk of developing type two diabetes (Leech, 2018.). Other benefits of olive oil include a high antioxidant count, which helps to neutralize harmful chemical processes in the body. It also has antibacterial properties, which help tackle problem bacteria in the stomach, and high levels of Oleic acid, which helps regulate our bodies processes. In addition, it has been proven to reduce inflammation and may even benefit genes linked to cancer.

The switch to olive oil is easy. Over time, you will provide your body the ability to help improve your mental and emotional health. Olive oil, by the way, is one example where moderation doesn't apply so much. Many experts even recommend having a shot or two of extra virgin olive oil daily.

There are many ways to maintain a solid core and, therefore, your resilience. I hope these few pointers guide you on your journey to a more balanced, calm approach to life. This last chapter has been fundamental and easy reminders, and sometimes you'll find that the most accessible steps are often the most life-changing.

Continue your practice of the five basics here:

- Remembering and acknowledging your capacity to grow and change.
- Not immediately reacting- calm mindfulness and meditation.
- Identify fear as the "thing" it is, letting it go from your newfound perspective of the transience of life.
- Remain grateful.
- Remain empathic.

The ideas contained in this book will enhance your daily life, and your strength will progress. I hope the building blocks I have provided keep you feeling as though you can come back from something that has hit you hard or prepare you for any potentially devastating occurrence with a steadfast and peaceful demeanor. Remember, you aren't the first, and you won't be the last to endure difficulties. You are part of the legion.

Maintain a healthy stance, and you will be able to manage what comes your way and be better in the end for it with calm resilience. I know this.

FINAL WORDS

Life isn't easy. No matter what we do, life has a habit of throwing curveballs in our direction from left, right, and center. No matter how we predict or prepare, things change against our will, and we can be left to pick up the emotional pieces of what once was.

In my life, things haven't always been as positive as they are now. Relationship breakdowns, financial ruin, and severe illness on the brink of death are all a part of my story. I learned the truths of life the hard way. So too, did I learn the most invaluable lesson: I learned the power of resilience.

Through heartache after heartache, my resilience has only made me stronger, and I hope you find the courage in yourself to grow as I have with the help of my findings in this book.

There is a bright side to your struggles; I am a testament to that. Pain and strife are inevitable, but don't let them define you or your story. You have the absolute power to overcome any adversity, no matter how impossible that may seem, and emerge from the other side as a more robust, braver, and more rounded individual. Life can and will be good again if you conjure the determination to make it so.

Fortify yourself before the storms head your way. Build your armor of resilience, and feel it protect you from future wounds and heal those of your past. Suffering is not an eternal, unending fact of your life, while change is. Suffering is merely part of your human experience, and this human experience, I reiterate, is constantly shifting. Get ready to experience joy again, and before you know it, you will be on the path to healing.

Let's recap.

Resilience is a crucial personality trait to nurture should you wish to experience the highs and lows of life with a steady and confident outlook. Remember to stretch your adaptability muscles, loosen them, and allow yourself to break free from the mold of your current mindset. With this freedom, you will find yourself adjusting to whatever life throws your way.

Your flexible mindset will help you to adapt to new situations with the inner knowledge that within yourself is the ability to face whatever struggles come your way. Our brains change – remember the concept of our brain's neuroplasticity? – so allow your mindset to adapt and let your innate ability to transform take the lead.

With this adaptability comes the growth mindset. You are more than capable of enhancing your growth mindset and implementing its benefits in your life, and with this mindset, you should see the beginnings of a new path to your future healing and success. Know you are continually growing and that the opportunities to grow present themselves to you every day; accept them head-on.

The effects of your childhood and childhood environment may still linger with you today, but awareness of how these things have affected your growth mindset is the first step in refusing to let them control your life any further.

How do we take control?

With calm mindfulness.

By gaining a more objective view of the world around us, and grounding ourselves in the realities of our body and environment, our emotions don't hold such a strong influence over our actions and reactions.

With this mindfulness comes the ability to remain calm in situations, not giving in to knee-jerk reactions. This new stance enables us to make better decisions and transform negative self-talk into positive, which will alter our sense of self and our understanding of what we are truly capable of withstanding. The dynamic nature of mindfulness promotes investigation of the world around you, transforming the attention of your thoughts from the abstract to the present. Live in the present as much as you can and feel your perspective shift.

This shift in perspective can help in repositioning your approach to fear. Remember that fear is a survival mechanism and is, for the most part, there to protect us. Sometimes fear and anxiety can be overwhelming, almost as if it's been set to override. Things that pose no direct danger can scare us to a point where daily tasks are made much more difficult. Learn to let go of your fears! The advice in this book (specifically chapter three) will guide you in relinquishing fear's control over your life.

Build your resilience even further by practicing gratitude and changing your perspective. By examining how we look at different situations from different points of view, we will learn how to create a healthier perspective that improves how we respond to traumatic events in our life.

At their very best, problems are a perfect opportunity for personal growth.

With practice and determination, we can permanently change how we view life. See these opportunities for growth and learning everywhere you look. But, of course, this won't eliminate the emotional effects of trauma, but a change of perspective helps us to deal with these emotions and heal in the most pertinent way. A change in perception will prompt newfound gratitude for the beauty you see in the world and even appreciation for the issues around you and their ability to transform you into the best version of yourself.

So, we have built our resilience following the steps and advice in the previous chapters. Now it's time to keep resilience part of everyday reality- as natural as breathing!

Make changes in your life concerning your new mindset, way of thinking, and perception of the world. The most important way you can do this is to reflect on the resilience, understanding, and empathy you've garnered through your crisis or trauma. Share your stories of failure and triumph and see the effects it has on your strength and understanding of life. You will find that people understand what you've been through and have even felt the same as you do now at some point in their lives. Use this connection to others to ease your loneliness and help these people feel understood in return. Nurturing the resiliency and strength in others will help you build these same traits in yourself.

There are many ways to maintain your resilience through the smaller tasks you can implement into your daily routine right here and now. Keep up your healthy mindset by practicing self-kindness and empathy, utilizing vision that can inspire you every day, and keeping up your physical health through a balanced diet, adequate sleep, and naps! And make sure to move whenever you can.

With all this book has to offer, I hope you find it within yourself to build your resilience to a point where you can tackle anything and everything that comes your way. Allow yourself to heal and find joy in life once again. Finding the freedom to embrace what is temporarily problematic or traumatic, turn it on its head, and bounce back better than you were before.

Time after time, resilience has carried me through crises and times of anguish until I have reached the other side, bruised but very much alive. I know that you have the power in yourself to nurture your resilience to the same life-changing effect. Let your resilience be your lifeline, not just for you but for others around you.

Now you have all the tools to enhance your resilience and improve your life experiences. Don't doubt yourself – know that you can not only "get through" challenging and terrible days but thrive as a result.

If you have found the information and testimonials in this book helpful, **please leave a review on Amazon.** I would love to hear your stories and how you became successful in owning your strength and becoming the resilient person that was always inside you!

Scan the QR code below for a quick review!

With immense gratitude, this book is dedicated to healthcare and mental healthcare workers everywhere. And to the experts at Yale who solved my deadly riddle in the nick of time; particularly the brilliant cardiac surgeon Dr Abeel Mangi and the team of 30+ skilled physicians, nurses, ICU specialists, social workers in the Center for Advanced Heart Failure. Thank you to Jay Meizlish for helping maintain health and good humor.

To the compassionate night nurse who, by sharing her struggles with panic attacks, helped allay my fears during a particularly long night's journey.

And lastly, to the self-sacrificing family, kind friends, and to Muggy, Sam and Kaeli, who have come shining through their dark days.

"Gratitude is the memory of the heart"

J.B. MASSIEU

RESOURCES

Introduction and Definition of Resilience

US Department of Veterans' Affairs https://www.ptsd.va.gov/2022

Ackerman, Courtney E., July 2018, *What is Neuroplasticity? A Psychologist Explains*, Positive Psychology, https://positivepsychology.com/neuro-plasticity/, date accessed: 29th September 2022

American Psychological Association, 2022, *Resilience*, APA, Washington DC, https://www.apa.org/topics/resilience, date accessed: 29th September 2022

American Psychological Association, August 2022, *Trauma*, APA, Washington DC, https://www.apa.org/topics/resilience, date accessed: 29th September 2022

BBC Bitesize, 2022, *Life and Teachings of the Buddha: the Four Noble Truths*, BBC, https://www.bbc.co.uk/bitesize/guides/zd8bcj6/revision/5, date accessed: 29th September 2022

https://earlyconnections.mo.gov/professionals/trauma-informed-care accessed November 23, 2022

Menezes Guimaraes, Daniel., Valerio-Gomez, Bruna., Lent, Roberto., November 2020, *Neuroplasticity: the Brain Changes Over Time!*, Frontiers, https://kids.frontiersin.org/articles/10.3389/frym.2020.522413, date accessed: 29th September 2022

https://www.frontiersin.org/articles/10.3389/fnbeh.2013.00010/full#B157 Behavioral Neuroscience Date accessed November 20 2022.

Batz, Carrie, 5th March 2018 *How Trauma Changes the Brain* https://www.theindependencecenter.org/how-trauma-changes-the-brain/ date accessed 20 November 2022

St. Joseph, Daniel., September 2020, *5 Ways to End Sufferings According to Buddhism*, Medium, https://medium.com/live-your-life-on-purpose/the-5-ways-to-end-sufferings-according-to-buddhism-6bc62332e945, date accessed: 29th September 2022

Chapter One

Stephens, Karen., 2007, *Parents are Powerful Role Models for Children*, Parenting Exchange, https://www.easternflorida.edu/community-resources/child-development-centers/parent-resource-library/docu ments/parents-powerful-role-models.pdf, date accessed: 29th September 2022

Therapist Aid, 2022, *Strengths-Based Therapy*, https://www.therapistaid. com/therapy-guide/strengths-based-therapy, date accessed: 29th September 2022

Rymanowicz, Kylie., January 2018, *The Nine Traits of Temperament: Adaptability*, Michigan State University, https://www.canr.msu.edu/ news/the_nine_traits_of_temperament_adaptability, date accessed: 29th September 2022

Southwick, S. M., and Charney, D. S. (2012). The science of resilience: implications for the prevention and treatment of depression. *Science* 338, 79–82. Rutter, M. (1993). Resilience: some conceptual considerations. *J. Adolesc. Health* 14, 626–631, 690–696.

https://www.frontiersin.org/articles/10.3389/fnbeh.2013.00010/ full#B157 Behavioral Neuroscience Date accessed November 20 2022.

Western Governor's University, April 2019, *What is a Growth Mindset? 8 Steps to Develop One*, https://www.wgu.edu/blog/what-is-growth-mindset-8-steps-develop-one1904.html#close, date accessed: 29th September 2022

Epstein, Mark., August 2013, *The Trauma of Everyday Life*, Penguin Random House, New York p 57.

Chapter Two

American Psychological Association, October 2019, *Mindfulness Meditation: A Research-Proven Way to Reduce Stress*, APA, Washington DC, https://www.apa.org/topics/mindfulness/meditation, date accessed: 3rd October 2022

Peterson, Tanya ChoosingTherapy. Org. "Mindfulness for Anxiety. How it Works and Techniques to Try" https://www.choosingtherapy.com/mindfulness-for-anxiety/

Epstein, Mark., August 2013, *The Trauma of Everyday Life*, Penguin Random House, New York

The Greater Good Science Centre, 2022, *What is Mindfulness?*, The University of California,https://greatergood.berkeley.edu/topic/mindfulness/definition, date accessed: 30th September 2022

James Madison University, 2022, *About Emotions*, James Madison University Education, https://www.jmu.edu/counselingctr/files/About%20Emotions.pdf, date accessed: 30th September 2022

Mindful Staff, July 2020, *What is Mindfulness?*, Mindful, https://www.mindful.org/what-is-mindfulness/, date accessed: 30th September 2022

Chapter Three

Brown, Les., January 2021, *Embrace Fear*, Les Brown Classics, Youtube, https://www.youtube.com/watch?v=4eGUI2T7k50, date accessed: 30th September 2022

Chodron, Pema., 1994, *Start Where You Are: A Guide To Compassionate Living*, Shambhala Classics, pg 23-24, pg 117-119

DeJohn, Kristin., March 2022, *Fight or Flight Response: What Is It, and How Does it Work?*, Ro, https://ro.co/health-guide/fight-or-flight-response/, date accessed: 30th September 2022

Fritscher, Lisa., September 2022, *What is Fear?*, Very Well Mind, https://www.verywellmind.com/the-psychology-of-fear-2671696, date accessed: 30th September 2022

National Alliance of Mental Illness, December 2017, *Anxiety Disorder*, NAMI, https://www.nami.org/About-Mental-Illness/Mental-Health-Conditions/Anxiety-Disorders date accessed: 30th September 2022

Segal, Elizabeth A., December 2020, *Conquering Fear*, Psychology Today, https://www.psychologytoday.com/us/blog/social-empathy/202012/conquering-fear, date accessed: 30th September 2022

Chapter Four

Barbash, Elyssa., January 2019, *The Power of Perspective Shift During Difficult Times*, Tampa Therapy, https://tampatherapy.com/2019/01/09/the-power-of-perspective-shift-during-difficult-times/, date accessed: 30th September 2022

Harvard Medical School, August 2021, *Giving Thanks Can Make You Happier*, Harvard Health Publishing, https://www.health.harvard.edu/healthbeat/giving-thanks-can-make-you-happier, date accessed: 30th September 2022

Hicks, Abraham., July 2019, *Appreciate Life's Contrast. BEST Description of What Life's Contrasting Experiences Mean*, Summer Song, https://www.youtube.com/watch?v=sXw-9bmn8Wc, date accessed: 8th October 2022

Hicks, Abraham., May 2021, *Feeling Appreciation Despite the Contrast*, Feel Good, https://www.youtube.com/watch?v=hcKkev7sCWs4, date accessed: 8th October 2022

Lovering, Nancy., March 2022, *Ten Ways to Help You Get Through Tough Times*, Pysch Central, https://psychcentral.com/health/how-to-get-through-hard-times#positive-projection, date accessed: 30th September 2022

Social Media Victims Law Centre, 2022, *Social Media's Effects on Self-Esteem*, https://socialmediavictims.org/mental-health/self-esteem/, date accessed: 30th September 2022

Chapter Five

Baker, Joe., December 2016, *A Call For Empathy: Key to Effective Communication and Relationships*, People Results, https://www.people-results.com/call-empathy-key-effective-communication-relation ships/, date accessed: 30th September 2022

Chodron, Pema., 1994, *Start Where You Are: A Guide To Compassionate Living*, Shambhala Classics, pg 67-68

De Waal, Frans., September 2009, *What Exactly is Empathy?*, Emory, https://www.emory.edu/LIVING_LINKS/empathy/faq.html, date accessed: 30th September 2022

Hawthorne, Hayley., Lowenbraun, Nicole., 2022, *10 Ways to Communicate With Empathy and Authority in Times of Crisis*, Duarte, https://www.d-uarte.com/presentation-skills-resources/impor tant-communicate-empathy-authority-times-crisis/, date accessed: 30th September 2022

Morrison, Elizabeth., October 2019, *Empathic Communication Companion Guide*, The California Institute for Behavioural Health Solutions, https://work.cibhs.org/sites/main/files/file-attachments/empathic_-communication_new_companion_guide_november_2019_final.pdf?1588608612, date accessed: 30th September 2022

Poulsen, Sophie., 2022, *Why Interpersonal Leadership Skills Matter and How to Improve*, THNK, https://www.thnk.org/blog/interpersonal-leader-ship-skills/, date accessed: 30th September 2022

Stevanovic, Melisa., Perakyla, Anssi., April 2015, *Experiences Sharing, Emotional Reciprocity, and Turn-Taking*, Frontiers, https://www.fron-tiersin.org/articles/10.3389/fpsyg.2015.00450/full, date accessed: 30th September 2022

Chapter Six

Leech, Joe., September 2018, *11 Proven Benefits of Olive Oil*, Health Line, https://www.healthline.com/nutrition/11-proven-benefits-of-olive-oil, date accessed: 30th September 2022

Napper, Paul., Rao, Anthony., April 2019, *Seven Ways to Feel More in*

Control of Your Life, The University of California, https://greater-good.berkeley.edu/article/item/seven_ways_to_feel_more_in_control_of_your_life, date accessed: 30th September 2022

Santos-Longhurst, Adrienne., August 2020, *What Is A Sugar Detox? Effects And How To Avoid Sugar*, Health Line, https://www.healthline.com/health/sugar-detox-symptoms#side-effects, date accessed: 11th October 2022